S0-ARF-534

Circle of Vines

Circle of Vines

THE STORY OF NEW YORK WINE

RICHARD FIGIEL

excelsior editions
State University of New York Press
Albany, New York

Published by State University of New York Press, Albany

© 2014 Richard Figiel

All rights reserved

Printed in the United States of America

No part of this book may be used or reproduced in any manner whatsoever without written permission. No part of this book may be stored in a retrieval system or transmitted in any form or by any means including electronic, electrostatic, magnetic tape, mechanical, photocopying, recording, or otherwise without the prior permission in writing of the publisher.

Excelsior Editions is an imprint of State University of New York Press

For information, contact State University of New York Press, Albany, NY
www.sunypress.edu

Production by Jenn Bennett
Marketing by Fran Keneston

Library of Congress Cataloging-in-Publication Data

Figiel, Richard.
    Circle of vines : the story of New York wine / Richard Figiel.
        pages cm
    Includes bibliographical references and index.
    ISBN 978-1-4384-5380-4 (pbk. : alk. paper)
    1. Wine and wine making—New York (State)—History. I. Title.

TP557.5.N7F54 2014
338.4'7663209747—dc23   2014002039

10 9 8 7 6 5 4 3 2 1

Contents

List of Illustrations

Map

Figures

Preface

If this book had one starting point, it was in a seedy trailer on the shoulder of Bully Hill, January 1978. I spent much of that winter trimming vines for Heron Hill Vineyards, though I had no experience pruning grapevines. The closest I'd come to vineyards was the sylvan pictures on the labels of bottles I'd written about for a wine magazine in New York City. The owner of Heron Hill, Pete Johnstone, didn't seem to care. "Just give them a haircut," he said. He had taken the same leap from city to Finger Lakes farm a decade earlier.

My workmate and roommate in the trailer, Vinnie Rizzo, had grown up on a fruit farm near Lake Ontario where his father grew grapes for the Taylor winery. Through a friend of Vinnie's at Taylor, our woodstove had access to a seemingly endless supply of oak stickers emptying out of the old Pleasant Valley champagne cellars; these were the wood slats used over the past century to stack millions of sparkling wine bottles in tierage. The wood burned like fossil-coal, but there was an unsettling chill embedded in its heat: we were fueling our fire with fragments of Keuka Lake wine's glorious past, at a time when things were falling apart. Coca-Cola had just acquired the Taylor Wine Company and the dismantling had begun.

At Heron Hill, instead of pruning the farm's old Delaware vines we ripped them out to replant with Riesling. The wine Johnstone made from his final harvest of Delaware in 1977 would later earn a swan-song gold medal at the state fair. We burned those vines too.

As the vineyards lost all their leaves and their pruned branches that winter, so the entire New York wine industry appeared to be dying before it could regenerate. I bought an abandoned Catawba vineyard on the next lake to the east and, like Johnstone, began pulling out the past to plant the future. One day as I was lining up end-posts for the rows of my new vineyard (it was a matter of pride to get them perfectly aligned, row to row), my eye wandered beyond the last post into scrubby woods on the slope below, and there amid the junipers and brambles was a fitful row of weather-beaten posts, ghosts of a vineyard on that hillside that predated the vineyard I'd pulled out to plant mine. I was looking back into the nineteenth century, and my posts happened to line up arrow-straight with that bleached, overgrown row of ghosts.

That sight probably made this book inevitable. I had latched onto the tail of a long story that needed to be explored and told. Part of the exploration involved a few decades of learning how to grow grapes on my Seneca farm, make wine from them, experiment with organic viticulture, wild-yeast fermentation, old ways of doing things.

In the research for this book I have depended, like Tennessee Williams's Blanche Dubois, on the kindness of strangers, as well as the generosity of friends. Some of the strangers have become friends in a shared enchantment with the past.

Members of the Underhill Society, especially Sarah and Robert "Woody" Underhill, were most helpful in retrieving the story of New York's first big vineyard at Croton Point. My thanks also to Marc Cheshire of the Friends of Croton Point, and Colleen Hughes at the Brotherhood winery.

In the Finger Lakes I am indebted to the candid insights of Fred Frank, to Gene Pierce, Carol and Jim Doolittle, Bruce Reisch and Alan Lakso at the Geneva Experiment Station, Kirk House and the diligent women volunteers of the Steuben County Historical Society, Rick Leisenring at the Glenn Curtiss Museum, Paul Sprague at the Greyton Taylor Wine Museum, Evan Fay Earle's navigation through the archives of Cornell's Kroch Library, and the generous swapping of notes by my colleague Thomas Pellechia. Special thanks to the administrator of Cornell's Lee Library in Geneva, Mike Fordon, who threw himself into my project as if it were his own.

The surprising history of wineries on the western edge of the Finger Lakes has come to light largely through the efforts of Gary Cox and Jane Oakes at the Town of York Historical Society, backed up by the archival detective work of Cornell librarian Marty Schlabach. My thanks also to one-time O-Neh-Da winemaker John Cicero, and in Chautauqua County to historian John Slater and winegrowers Jennifer and Fred Johnson, Jr.

For their help with the inspiring story of Long Island wine, many thanks to Steve Mudd, Chris Baiz, Louisa Hargrave, Larry Perrine, Alice Wise at Cornell's Riverhead research station, and Mariella Ostroski at the Cutchogue New Suffolk Free Library.

For all its ups and downs, the story of New York wine has barely begun; in the millennial time-scale of winemaking, this region is still in the nursery. To create a snapshot of how this state has plowed into the twenty-first century, many other people unnamed above have also contributed, not least my wife Deborah Pfautsch who, after years enduring my harangues about this project, still volunteered to go through it all again, producing the index.

Trumansburg, 2013

CHAPTER 1

Prehistory

*About 10,000 years ago the wall of ice departed northern New York.
It left behind a landscape that quickly came back to life. Fast-growing
plants like grapevines were early colonizers; wild grapes repopulated
nearly every corner of the state. The prospects for commercial viticulture
would be another matter.*

On the North Fork of Long Island some vineyards wash against a line
of bluffs that hold back Long Island Sound and the ocean. When
tractors till vine rows skirting those bluffs, their discs may stir up
cobbles of granite that by all rights belong on 2,000-foot Berkshire
mountaintops, 100 miles away.

Along the slopes rimming the Finger Lakes, growers also run discs
through vineyards, sometimes peeling up scrims of shale imprinted with
the shapes of ocean creatures–scallop shells, trilobites, brachiopods,
sometimes fragments of the shells themselves–200 miles from the sea.
Grape-growing pioneers in the Thousand Islands district of the St.
Lawrence River Valley and on Lake Champlain might keep an eye
out for shards of whale bone.

The vineyards of New York are where they are, partly due to
these anomalies in the ground underfoot. To flourish, vineyards need
well-drained sites like the coarse stones and sand on Long Island or
the crumbly shale of the Finger Lakes. Limestone deposits left from the
shells of ancient sea creatures give some wines an edge of complexity.
The geologic curiosities that turn up in New York's vineyards give us

clues about how the land has created microclimates that ripen grapes slowly, bringing subtlety and balance to wine.

Fully appreciating New York's unique viticultural heritage requires a quick look back in time, beginning as far back as the era of earth's supercontinent Pangaea. The earliest fossils of the plant genus "vitis"– the grapevine–date from the time of that single land mass more than 200 million years ago. When continents separated, vitis also split onto distinct eastern and western evolutionary paths, accounting for vivid differences between the flavors, aromas, and cultural habits of North American and European (vinifera) grapes. As it colonized divergent habitats, the genus fragmented into many species adapting to varied topography, soils, and climates. North America suited the plant particularly well, inviting it into nearly every temperate corner of the land, especially east of the Rocky Mountains. Of the perhaps 60-odd species of grapevine identified worldwide (the number is in dispute), almost three-quarters are native to North America. A half dozen of those grow wild in New York State, most notably vitis Riparia, Aestivalis, and Labrusca.

Millions of years ago much of what would be western, central, and northern New York lay under a shallow lobe of the ocean. It pulsed with rising and falling sea levels, collecting run-off from Acadian mountains to the east–layer upon layer upon layer of mud and sand spread across the sea bottom, liberally sprinkled with marine animal shells.

As the inland sea eventually receded, its bottom sediments compacted into the stratification of shale and limestone that underlie central and western New York. Over this emerging plain, river systems drained north and south. The lines of the Finger Lakes were once the upper reaches of those rivers; Keuka Lake's slingshot shape records the confluence of two tributaries.

This was the landscape that glaciers descended upon in the last Ice Age, the geologic event that shaped the state we know from Lake Erie to the tip of Long Island and the top of Lake Champlain. A mantle of ice more than a mile high moved over the land at about a meter a day. It covered the highest peaks of ancient Adirondacks, causing a spectacular alteration of topography. Trees, soil, boulders were bulldozed for scores of miles. Where they encountered valleys, the vanguards of ice channeled into lobes: one down the Champlain-

Hudson corridor (with a spur along the Mohawk), another down the Black River Valley, others following the western river valleys–gouging out deep troughs.

It was a halting assault. Ice advanced, retreated, advanced again as earth's temperature fluctuated. Where it paused at the end of each surge it dumped a moraine: massive quantities of debris like the lines of seaweed left on a beach after high tide. The furthest advance south occurred around 22,000 years ago, drawing a line through northern Pennsylvania and New Jersey and dropping its terminal moraine as Staten and Long Islands. Long Island actually consists of two moraines, distinct on the east end as the North and South Forks but overlapping to the west. New York's ocean island is not, after all, an overzealous sandbar but rather a colossal, 120-mile-long, glacial dump–a mélange of silt, sand, gravel, and rocks courtesy of upstate New York and New England.

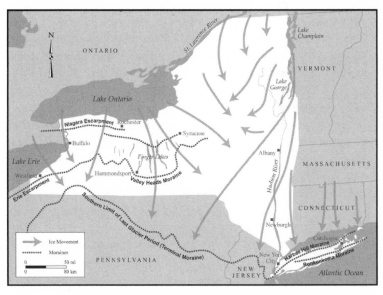

MAP 1.1. The most recent surge of glaciers across New York State came and went in waves that reached farthest south around 25,000 years ago. In the ice sheet's 15,000 years of fitful retreat, it shaped the terrain that governs the growing of New York wine. (*Map by Matthew Bazylewskyj*)

The ice lobe making its way down the Hudson Valley cut a trench deepening at about the present location of Troy and creating what is essentially a fjord through the Hudson Highlands. The depth of the river channel allows ocean tides and with them the warming influence of a maritime climate to penetrate north as far as Albany. Salt water reaches Poughkeepsie, regularly pushing the upper Hudson backwards—a river that flows both ways.

In the central part of the state, the glacial moraine most significant in shaping modern topography was deposited during the ebb and flow of the ice sheet's retreat. The Valley Heads moraine is easily traced today along the southern ends of Finger Lakes, where dumped debris plugged up old river valleys. The extraordinary depth of modern Seneca and Cayuga Lakes—the bottoms of both fall well below sea level—tells us those were the two largest rivers channeling the flow of ice.

Meltwater accumulating along the front of the receding ice sheet formed gigantic postglacial lakes that remained for thousands of years. Lake Albany filled the Hudson Valley from the terminal moraine at Staten and Long Islands to Glens Falls. It eventually punched through the moraine at Verrazano Narrows and drained into the ocean, leaving sediments of mud and sand. Another postglacial lake filled the valley between New York and Vermont, leaving sandy beach lines well up into the Adirondack foothills as it dwindled down to become remnant Lake Champlain.

By far the largest of these meltwater lakes spread across central and western New York, over the plain once covered by inland sea. The Finger Lakes, Lake Oneida, Lakes Erie and Ontario are all remnants of what geologists call Lake Iroquois. The gravel terraces stepping down from the escarpments along both Erie and Ontario record sudden drops in the level of Lake Iroquois as ice dams holding back meltwater periodically gave way.

About 10,000 years ago the wall of ice departed northern New York. It left behind a landscape that gradually came back to life. Fast-growing plants like grapevines were early colonizers; wild grapes repopulated nearly every corner of the state.

The prospects for commercial viticulture are another matter. Much of interior New York is too cold to ripen grapes reliably enough for a profitable farm, with a growing season too short and winter-low temperatures dropping too far below zero. Searching out more temperate microclimates is the first order of business for aspiring grape-growers. Slope and aspect to the sun can be critical. Good water drainage is essential, grapevines being notoriously intolerant of "wet feet." And everywhere soil composition enters into the equation behind good wine.

Erie and Ontario

In the Erie-Chautauqua district, the ridge-line paralleling Lake Erie's shore crests from 500 to 1,000 feet above the lake's surface. Alluvial clay soils at water's edge give way to gravel along beach-line terraces, then outcrops of shale at the face of the escarpment.

The undulating, easily worked mid-section became New York State's home for the Concord grape. In his 1907 magnum opus, *The Grapes of New York*, horticulturist U. P. Hedrick suggests the leaner shale loams on the side of the ridge promise the best wine while the deep, richer soil of the lake plain produces higher yields. In any case the most important role played by the escarpment is to capture and contain the climatic benefits of the lake: taking the edge off winter-low temperatures, holding back spring vine growth until after late frosts, homogenizing night and day temperatures in summer, lengthening the growing season and delaying fall frosts.

The escarpment hovers between one and a few miles from the lake. It comes closest and contains the strongest microclimatic influence around Westfield. All winter-bets are off, though, when the shallow lake freezes over.

Along the southern shore of Lake Ontario the Niagara escarpment sits farther back from the water, from four to nine miles, crossing the Niagara River at Lewiston and running east through Rochester. Ridge Road (Route 104) rides beach lines below the ridge like a surfer on the face of a wave. The climate dynamic is similar to Erie-Chautauqua, somewhat more diffused because it spreads over a wider area, but more reliable every winter because the deeper water of Ontario stays open. The gravelly soil of this lake plain has a higher limestone content, shared with the neighboring vineyards of Canada's Niagara Peninsula and with nearby northern Finger Lakes.

Finger Lakes

Indian legend tells us the lakes fill the imprint of the Great Spirit's hands, an account that rings true when we imagine those hands bearing down with fingers of ice. The depth of the trenches they scraped out has left slices of water, large volumes with narrow surfaces, creating a relatively stable core water temperature—in Seneca Lake, about 40 degrees year-round. The bottoms of Seneca and Cayuga Lakes fall well below sea level, containing bodies of water that virtually never ice-over even when air temperatures drop below zero. On such a day, funnels of vapor skitter along the lake surface as if frantically seeking a warm spot. As they radiate stored heat to enclosing hillsides, the lakes make viticulture possible in an inland region otherwise off limits. January–February temperatures are often 10 to 15 degrees warmer near the open lakes compared to half a mile away.

Like Erie and Ontario, the Finger Lakes also cushion the transitions of spring and fall. If temperatures briefly spike up in spring when vines are still dormant, the cooling influence of nearby water holds back impatient buds and tender new vine shoots until the risk of late frost passes. In fall the effect reverses, and the lakes give warmth to ripening grapes, sometimes postponing first frosts into November when the trees on surrounding hills are bare.

Long, even slopes along the lakes suggest a consistent soil profile. Not so. The glacial rearrangement of furniture left soils around the Finger Lakes extremely and abruptly variable; pH values veer from quite acid to alkaline. Ancient lakes and seabeds tended to leave more calcium from marine deposits in the flatter north, but glaciers smeared limestone down the valleys in erratic patterns. Patches of gravelly till pop up amid prevailing shale, which can be brittle and webbed with fractures that let vine roots go exploring, or the shale can turn thick and forbidding.

Hudson Valley

The Hudson River region presents viticulture with the state's most complex set of both opportunities and challenges. Opportunity comes with the valley's general climate: more sunny days than any of the state's

FIGURE 1.1. A vineyard behind the Bully Hill winery perches atop an excavated bank, revealing a subterranean profile typical of the Finger Lakes: a modest bed of soil over countless layers of crumbly shale, sandstone, and limestone from sediment at the bottom of an ancient sea. Vine roots feel their way down through fissures, sipping dissolved minerals, until they hit thick horizontal walls.

other grape areas; also a somewhat drier growing season as Taconic hills shield the area from some of the Atlantic moisture moving inland; and above all, the warming effect of maritime air channeled upriver.

The challenges come with the valley's turbulent topography. This is geologically wild country. The Hudson Highlands slash diagonally across the river around Cold Spring. To the north, shale and limestone recall the sedimentation in postglacial Lake Albany. To the south the highlands are made of the hard gneiss and granite that appear elsewhere mainly in the Adirondacks. The soils derived from these different rocks are more variable in the Hudson Valley than in any other New York vineyard district. The rolling terrain adds a second kaleidoscope of microclimates created by shifting degrees of slope, aspects to the sun, and presentations to the river.

Long Island

Natural phenomena that worry grape growers upstate—deep freezes, slope and air drainage, water drainage, rocky outcrops, abruptly changing soil types—not much of this bothers on Long Island. Deep glacial till and the warm embrace of the Atlantic on one side, the Sound on the other, Peconic Bay in the middle, make this in many ways New York's most comfortable base for viticulture. The island's maritime climate is moderately sunny. Atlantic sea breezes brush the low profile of the East End, tempering summer heat waves and helping to flush mildew and rot out of vine canopies.

There are modest differences between the viticultural potential of the island's two forks. Offshore breezes and fog banks tend to keep the South Fork a bit cooler, with a somewhat shorter ripening season. North Fork soil can be a little lighter, drier, warmer, opening more possibilities for red grape varieties.

The same ocean embrace that usually protects Long Island's East End from crop-threatening frosts and vine-threatening winter freezes also brings a hug of humidity that increases disease pressure. A less persistent but more potent threat comes periodically with coastal hurricanes, lashing land that dangles out in the sea. The storm season unfortunately coincides with the time when ripening grapes are most vulnerable, but even when storms come early, salt spray carried by withering winds can defoliate vines.

FIGURE 1.2. The nearly level North Fork of Long Island lifts gently up to a line of bluffs skirting Long Island Sound in the distance. They are the worn remains of the Harbor Hill moraine, deposited by glaciers giving birth to the island. Vineyards like the well-drained soil of outwash spilled from the moraine as the ice sheet melted. *(Courtesy of the Long Island Wine Council)*

There are some issues in the ground as well. Long Island's sandy-gravelly soil is so well-drained it dries out quickly in droughts, calling for irrigation on an island where the fresh-water aquifer is precious, threatened by development. And the East End's naturally acidic soil composition, without manipulation, is unfriendly to the European vinifera grape species, the only grapes islanders want to grow. For many reasons, what looks like New York's warmest climate for growing wine is not necessarily the easiest.

CHAPTER 2

Beginnings in the Hudson Valley

Although they have several times attempted to plant vineyards, and have not immediately succeeded, they, nevertheless, have not abandoned the hope of doing so by and by, for there is always some encouragement, although they have not as yet discovered the cause of the failure.

The first written record of the land we now call New York comes to us from the sixteenth-century journal of Giovanni da Verrazzano, a Florentine navigator who, like other explorers after Columbus, viewed the North American continent as a troublesome impediment in a trade route to the Orient.

In 1524 a group of French merchants and Italian bankers hired Verrazzano, with the blessing of King Francis I of France, to find a navigable passage through America. Having previously captured several Spanish galleons returning with plunder from Mexico, Verrazzano was on Spain's most-wanted list and steered clear of Spanish Florida, making landfall to the north in an area still uncharted. His journal soon begins describing a profusion of grapevines vaulting into treetops, with tantalizing prospects for wine. These were probably the wild Muscadine grapes native to the South.

As he followed the coast north and the climate shifted to favor the labrusca species of wild grapes, the vines receded deeper into the forest and disappeared entirely from his journal by the time he reached New York harbor. Verrazzano was the first European to record seeing it. He describes a deep river forcing its way to the sea through steep hills—the hills of Staten Island and Brooklyn that would be linked four and a half centuries later by a bridge bearing his name. As he entered the big harbor it came alive with canoes of wondering natives, but he barely had time to look around; chased out not by unfriendly Indians but by unfavorable winds.

It is hard to comprehend how it could take nearly another century before New York harbor and its river would again be described by Europeans. Religious strife consumed much of Europe's attention through the sixteenth century while Spain was busy sacking the great cultures of Mexico, and Central and South America. The search for a shorter water route to the Orient was still in force when Henry Hudson set sail from the Netherlands in 1609 with a crew of 16, half Dutch, half English, in the *Halve Maen*, more of a boat than a ship. He was a seasoned English navigator hired by Dutch merchants to find a channel to the East across the top of Russia, which he set out to do but then changed his plan and headed instead for North America, on a rogue mission to find the elusive passage west.

Perhaps with Verrazzano's map in hand, Hudson made his way to the New York harbor in September 1609, two years after the Virginia Company had landed settlers at Jamestown. The journal of Hudson's first mate Robert Juet tells us they proceeded upriver and soon "the people of the Countrie came flocking aboard, and brought us Grapes, and Pompions [squash], which we bought for trifles . . . And many brought us Beuers [beavers] skinnes, and Otters skinnes," an exchange that predicted the economics of New Netherlands for years to come.

Here as elsewhere in first contacts with Europeans, Native Americans showed they had no previous experience with alcohol derived from grapes or anything else. Hudson brought chiefs aboard ship and "gave them so much wine and Aqua vita, that they were all merrie . . . In the end one of them was drunke . . . and that was strange to them for they could not tell how to take it."

Hudson was carried upriver by the surge of tides, the persistence of salt water, and rope readings indicating a very deep channel, intimations of a link to the Oriental ocean, but in time the encouraging signs gave out. The *Half Moon* turned back at shallows north of present-day Albany on September 22. At almost the same time, Hudson's French arch-rival, the explorer Samuel de Champlain, was canoeing up Lake

Champlain 70 miles to the north—a Frenchman and an Englishman nearly meeting in the North American wilderness at a place that would mark the front lines of conflict between their two nations for 150 years to come.

Hudson worked for the Dutch East India Company, entrepreneurs primarily interested not in colonization but in trade. This would be the defining characteristic of New Netherlands—as it has arguably remained for New York City: the primacy of foreign trade over local subsistence. With apparently no northwest passage, the company quickly shifted its interest from the spices of Asia to North American furs, and the reclusive beaver found itself atop the coat-of-arms of a trading post at New Amsterdam.

When the first Dutch ship arrived with the intention of permanent settlement, in 1623, it found a French ship at anchor in the mouth of the river, just arrived and about to renew Verrazzano's claim for France. With two small cannons the Dutch ran the French out. Had those cannons been on the French ship instead, how differently the story of New York wine might have begun. The Dutch were beer makers; if they cultivated anything it would first be grains.

Even so, the abundance of wild grapevines was inspiring. Writing in Old Amsterdam in 1624, a Dutch merchant named Wassanaers expressed a trader's fantasy: "Vines grow wild there; were there vintagers and were they acquainted with the press, good wine could be brought hither [to the Netherlands] in great quantity, and even as Must, the voyage thence being often made in thirty days." He imagined a mobile winery, making the product as it was brought to market (and no need to stir the must)! Alas, there were no vintagers acquainted with the press.

A generation later, in a report to the home government on developments at New Amsterdam, the Dutch settlers were still marveling at the cornucopia of wild grapes and still only ruminating about making wine: "Almost the whole country, as well the forests as the maize lands and flats, is full of vines, but principally—as if they had been planted there—around and along the banks of the brooks, streams and rivers . . . The grapes are of many varieties; some white, some blue . . . their juice is pleasant and some of it white, like French or Rhenish Wine; that of others a very deep red, like Tent; some even paler; the vines run far up the trees and are shaded by their leaves, so that the grapes are slow in ripening and a little sour, but were cultivation and knowledge applied here, doubtless as fine Wines would then be made as in any other wine growing countries."

When the wine was made, however, even with cultivation and knowledge applied, the naturally high acidity, low sugar content, and tough skins of native grapes produced sour, harsh-tasting wine. It became clear these vines were of another order from the vineyards of the Old World.

The earliest record of an attempt to grow European grapevines in New Netherlands dates from 1642, when the patroon Kiliaen Van Rensselaer sent cuttings to his little colony near Fort Orange (Albany). His commissary reported they were soon killed by the frost. The cuttings had probably been sent for by Adriaen van der Donck, who ran the patroon's manor.

Van der Donck was the first lawyer to settle in New Netherland, a man with refined taste and a keen interest in wine. He eventually moved to land north of Manhattan island and published, in the 1650s, a *Description of the New-Netherlands* that includes a long, hopeful section on grapes and wine, concluding, "Within the last few years, the lovers of the vineyard have paid more attention to the cultivatiion of the vine . . . They have also introduced foreign stocks, and they have induced men to come over from Heidelberg who are vine dressers . . . Several persons already have vineyards and wine hills under cultivation . . . it is expected that in a few years there will be wine in abundance in the New-Netherlands."

Some historians have assumed seventeenth-century French Huguenots introduced vineyards and winemaking to the colony in their settlements at New Paltz or New Rochelle, but the Huguenots emigrated mainly from Belgium (the Walloons) or from Normandy and France's grape-less northern provinces, bringing with them fruit trees, apparently not grapevines. Hard cider, perry, and brandy were all made in the early years of New Netherlands from tree fruits. After England took control of the colony in 1664, one of the early English governors, Thomas Dongan, laid out a two-acre garden along the Broadway road in lower Manhattan. It was known as "Governor's Vineyard," located on what would later become the front lawn of City Hall. Dongan was a wine-lover; whether he ever drank his own wine is not known.

A pair of Netherlanders—Jasper Dankers and Peter Sluyter—spent the better part of 1679 traveling throughout the province of New York looking for a site to establish a utopian community. Dankers was a wine merchant, able to cast an analytical eye on the scene as they tramped through Brooklyn to visit Coney Island: "We discovered on the roads several kinds of grapes still on the vines, called speck grapes, which are not always good, and these were not; although they were sweet in the mouth at first, they made it disagreeable and stinking. The small blue grapes are better, and their vines grow in good form. Although they [colonists] have several times attempted to plant vineyards, and have not immediately succeeded, they, nevertheless, have not abandoned the hope of doing so by and by, for there is always some encouragement, although they have not as yet discovered the cause of the failure."

This illuminating bit of observation sums up the experience typical of colonists trying to grow imported European grape varieties: at first they seemed to grow well ("always some encouragement") but then mysteriously collapsed before producing much fruit—an exasperating scenario repeated over and over from John Smith's first years at the Jamestown settlement, John Winthrop's attempts to grow European grapes at Massachusetts Bay, Lord Delaware's in Virginia, Lord Baltimore's in Maryland, William Penn's at Philadelphia. The dream of American wine-vineyards powered what would be a long-term struggle against tiny insects and diseases unknown in Europe.

Importing wines by sail from Europe was risky and expensive. Without the ability to make their own good wine, American colonists directed their thirst instead to hard cider, brandy, cheap rum from the West Indies, and fortified Madeira from the island weigh-station on the trans-Atlantic trade route. Drunkenness was a huge problem in New Netherlands and old New York. The mercantile roots of the colony drew in a motley mix of nationalities, risk-takers, adventurers, wheeler-dealers and miscellaneous profligates; this was no Puritan city on a hill. The streets were lined with taverns and overrun with free-range pigs. Local authorities were continually issuing regulations and crack-downs with little effect. " 'Tis in this Country a common thing even for the meanest persons so soon as the bounty of God has furnished them with a plentiful crop to turne what they can as soon as may be into mony & that mony into drinke at the Same time when their family at home have nothing but rags to protect their bodies from the Winters cold," complained John Miller in his 1695 treatise, *New York Considered and Improved.* "Nay if the fruits of their plantations be such as are by their own immediate labour convertible into liquor such as Sider Perry &c they have scarce the patience to stay till it is fit for drinking but inviting their pot-companions they all of them neglecting whatsoever worke they are about set to it together & give not over till they have drank it off."

A sobering picture, still without the European tradition of wine in moderation with meals.

In the 1730s, Robert Prince began elaborating on a private garden nursery overlooking Flushing Bay, across the East River from Manhattan in Queens County. It would grow into an enterprise with enormous impact on the development of the grape and wine culture of New York State and beyond, through four generations of the Prince family. At the core of the garden were European fruit trees and plants collected from Belgian and French Huguenot settlers across Long Island Sound at New Rochelle.

Robert's son William Prince expanded his father's plantings into America's first successful commercial nursery around 1750. By the start of the American Revolution it covered eight acres and achieved such high regard that English General Lord Howe posted guards around the property during the British occupation of New York. Afterward, in 1789, newly elected President George Washington and Vice-President John Adams toured the Prince gardens, the source of fruit for their executive mansions in New York. A third-generation William Prince, Jr. tripled the nursery's acreage in 1793 and christened it the Linnaean Botanic Gardens, after the great Swedish botanist. Thomas Jefferson was an enthusiastic patron, buying plants for Monticello and sending many of the shrubs and flowers collected on the Lewis and Clark Expedition to Flushing for cataloging and propagation.

William Jr. and his son William Robert Prince put equal energy into experiments cultivating native plants and those testing the adaptability of exotics from Europe and Asia, with an increasing interest in grapes. They imported and tested more than 200 European grape varieties over a period of nearly 50 years, with the usual discouragement, finally giving up on commercial recommendation of the foreigners and concentrating on vines from American sources. Father and son published, in 1830, A Treatise on the Vine, the first comprehensive, scholarly book on grape culture in America. It included detailed instructions for planting, trellising, pruning, burying tender varieties for winter protection, smoking and spraying against insects and disease; it introduced the fungicide lime-sulfur; and it described scores of European and native grapes.

At the head of this list was a grape variety called Isabella, a new grape originally from South Carolina. It was propagated, promoted, and disseminated from the Linnaean nursery to growers around New York, to many other states, and even exported to Madeira and Europe (it would eventually become the most widely grown grape variety in the world). The nursery had obtained cuttings of the variety in 1816 from General Benjamin Gibbs, one of many backyard botanists in New York's garden districts of Queens and Brooklyn. The grape was named after the general's wife. Prince wrote "I have made wine from it of excellent quality, and which has met with the approbation of some of the most accurate judges in our country."

The Linnaean nursery list featured another new grape from the South called Catawba. Like Isabella it was the product of random pollination between an imported European vine, during the seasons before it succumbed, with a nearby wild American plant. These two grape varieties—Isabella and Catawba—would enable and dominate the early viticulture of New York.

At the time of A Treatise on the Vines's publication, the Linnaean Botanic Garden was growing 450 varieties of grapes. William Robert Prince described the challenges of sorting through their different permutations, including "varieties of original native species, varieties obtained by admixture of native species, varieties obtained from seeds of exotic grapes, varieties obtained by admixture of foreign and native varieties." Grapes still represented a small fraction of the plants offered in the Linnaean catalogue. The depth of the Princes' experimentation made their Flushing nursery the nation's central clearinghouse for horticultural plants and for information on where and how to grow them, but it was hardly alone supplying new vines to New York and beyond.

A winegrower from southern France, Alphonse Loubat, emigrated to Brooklyn in the 1820s accompanied by several thousand three-year-old grapevines. He planted them on a slope above Gravesend Bay in the old Dutch village of New Utrecht and promoted his new nursery business with a little manual bravely entitled *The American vine-dresser's guide*, 1827. It was printed alternately in French and English on facing pages, on the assumption that French grapes and vineyard practices could simply be transposed onto American soil. His nursery vineyard grew to 40 acres containing over 150,000 imported vines. He supplied vines to Nicholas Longworth in Ohio when Longworth was experimenting with European vines to build what would become America's first major commercial wine venture. But both Longworth and Loubat struggled desperately against diseases and bugs unknown in France. Longworth gave up on European vinifera vines and replanted with Catawba. Loubat was driven to tying paper bags around his precious clusters to protect them, in vain.

Alphonse Loubat was a fervent admirer of Benjamin Franklin. The *vine-dresser's guide* was dedicated "To the Shade of Franklin," asking his spirit to "Protect my feeble essay . . . [and] my vine, and cause it so to thrive that I shall soon be able to pour forth upon thy tomb libations of perfumed Muscatel." Alas, the great man's spirit was no more help than the paper bags. Loubat sold his New Utrecht property for building lots and returned to France in 1835. But like Franklin he was a man with many interests and an inventive mind and before he left, even as he toiled in the vineyard, he designed the configuration of recessed rails for Manhattan's first streetcar system.

The editor of Brooklyn's leading newspaper *The Long Island Star*, Alden Spooner, was a keen observer of Loubat's venture, to the point of planting his own little block of 50 French and German vines. It was located in what later became Prospect Park. Like Loubat's, Spooner's European vines soon surrendered to rot. But unlike Loubat he had also planted Isabella vines purchased from Prince in 1827, and they flourished. He made a barrel of wine from his first crop in 1831 and sent samples to 50 interested friends and colleagues, with encouraging feedback. The following year he made eight barrels, experimenting with various methods and uneven success (this is the earliest specific record of a substantial amount of wine made in New York). In his capacity as a prominent journalist Spooner did much to popularize the culture of grapes and wine in the New York area and beyond, eventually publishing an engaging meditation with many practical tips, *The Cultivation of American Grape Vines & Making of Wine* (1846).

Another Frenchman, actually a French-speaking Belgian, ran another influential European-grape nursery in Brooklyn not far from Loubat's, at the intersection of two old Dutch roads that would become Flatbush and Jamaica Avenues. Andre Parmentier wrote a letter to *The New England Farmer* announcing, "I have imported the last year 20,000 vine roots covering 4 acres of my establishment which includes 24 acres." In the middle of his "Horticultural Garden" he built a rustic observation tower. It provided a raven's-eye view of the familiar scenario: a few years of promising growth, then relentless decline.

During the vineyard's initial tease of success, Parmentier's nursery, like Loubat's, fed European-variety vines to many would-be winegrowers, from gardeners with glass topiaries, where the vines often succeeded in hermetic environments, to entrepreneurial farms, where they always failed. One of Parmentier's customers was Robert Underhill, the owner of a unique bulb of land extending into the Hudson River above Tarrytown—Croton Point. Warmed by the maritime influence coming upriver, it seemed an ideal site, but not for European vines. Within a few years Underhill pulled them out and replanted with Isabella and Catawba, purchased from the Prince nursery in 1827.

Across the river from Croton a French émigré, Thomas Gimbrede, taught drawing to cadets at the U.S. Military Academy while he experimented with grapevines. He had come to America in 1802, working as a dancing master, an engraver, and a miniature portraitist in New York City before taking the job at West Point. On walks in the surrounding woods he became enchanted by the sight of grapevines snaking through the trees, something not seen in France. He researched the different species growing wild, began collecting cuttings and rooted them in his garden, wondering if he could domesticate them into a proper French vineyard. If French vines refused to become American, perhaps American vines could learn to become more French. He spent the last 12 years of his life pruning down, manuring, and generally pampering his corralled wild vines, but the fruit they produced never lost its coarse flavors and puckering acidity.

Gimbrede's story was a particularly poignant example of ongoing, dogged efforts undertaken all over the country, from the backwoods to botanical gardens, searching for some way to make good wine in America. Even as his experiment proved to be one more failure, a breakthrough was underway with the appearance of the two new American grape varieties, Catawba and Isabella, and their dissemination by the Princes' Linnaean nursery in the 1820s.

The Underhill plantation on Croton Point is considered New York State's first successful commercial vineyard. Robert Underhill was an ambitious, nimble businessman with an eye on upscale marketing opportunities in nearby New York City. During the War of 1812, when the city was cut off from the South by a British blockade, he grew 80 acres of watermelons on his river-coddled peninsula to keep city folks supplied with their favorite Southern treat. Later he started manufacturing bricks, grew Newtown Pippin apples for export and castor bean plants for castor oil. When European grapes didn't work out for wine, he revised the plan to grow grapes for New York's fresh fruit market.

Underhill's sons, William and Richard, inherited the Croton Point estate in 1829 just as the replanted vineyard came into bearing. William's son Stephen took an interest in grapes and hybridizing new varieties, including one he named Croton. William turned from farming to run the family brickyard, supplying material for a new aqueduct connecting the Croton Reservoir to New York City. His brother Richard, a physician in the city, took charge of the vineyard. Over the next three decades he expanded the Croton Point vineyard to more than 50 acres. Richard Underhill was pushing the unconventional notion that grapes could be eaten as fresh fruit. He was the first American doctor to promote the so-called Grape Cure, fashionable in Europe, prescribing a diet of five pounds of grapes a day to ward off a constellation of ailments. Until the Cure, European tradition held that grapes were the beneficent source of wine or perhaps dried for raisins, but hardly candidates for eating fresh. The ebullient flavors of Croton Point's Isabella and Catawba helped change the way people viewed grapes.

FIGURE 2.1. Trade cards advertised the sale of a dozen vintages left in the Underhill cellars after the winery closed in 1871. Vines growing on Croton Point directly above the brick-arched vaults were abandoned, marking the end of New York's first commercial vineyard. (*Reprinted from the collection of Marc Cheshire*)

By the late 1850s Dr. Underhill had given up his medical practice and begun making wine, again with a medicinal pitch for "the pure product of the grape, neither drugged, liquored, nor watered, recommended by leading physicians in all cases where a stimulant of a bracing character is required." He was distancing himself from the common practices of adulterating imported wines and fortifying domestic wines with brandy. *The Christian Advocate* newspaper approved: "Dr. Underhill seems to have some conscience on the subject, for, not only does he steadily refuse to allow any drugged wines to be produced on his place—though he might do so to profit—he also refuses to have the refuse of his presses made into brandy, though probably ten per cent of the whole vintage is left in the pomace which is thrown away." Winemakers at the time routinely used additions of brandy as a preservative.

A row of caves dug into the south shore of Croton Point supplied table wines by steamship to New York City pharmacies, groceries, churches, and hotels. They were featured on menus of the Astor House and served at the wedding breakfast of Queen Victoria. But when Richard Underhill died in 1871, the business was paralyzed by feuding heirs. For six years 30,000 gallons of wine sat undisturbed in the Croton Point caves, until finally put on the market at fire-sale prices. The vineyards were abandoned; only the vaulted cave entrances remained to stare out at the river.

Croton Point had the Hudson Valley's first commercially successful vineyard but not its first winery. That milestone belongs across the river in Orange County at the village of Little York, later renamed Washingtonville. A 19-year-old shoemaker from Plainfield, New Jersey, named John Jaques settled there in 1809, built his cobbler business up into a general store, and planted a half acre of Catawba and Isabella grapevines (from the Prince nursery) in the backyard. It soon oversupplied the store. He tried sending his grapes to market in New York but he was competing with Underhill; Washingtonville was ten miles from the river, and hauling costs ate up Jaques's profits. He began experimenting with fermentation. In the 1830s he laid out a 10-acre vineyard on a ridge at the edge of town, hand-dug a small cellar, and in 1839 the Jaques Winery produced the Hudson Valley's first commercial vintage.

From the beginning and for many years the wines were sold mainly to churches. When opportunities for store sales came along, John Jaques, the cobbler son of Scottish New Jerseyites, became *Jean Jaques*, the French vigneron, on wine labels. John's sons took over by 1859 when a Jaques Brothers Winery flyer offered "wines made from Isabella, Catawba and the newer varieties of our native Grapes"— Delaware and Concord grapes had just debuted in the Hudson Valley.

By the time the last surviving Jaques brother sold the winery to New York City wine merchants Jesse and Edward Emerson, in 1886, the

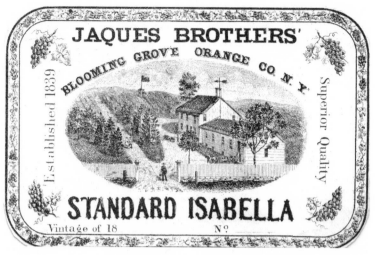

FIGURE 2.2. An early label shows the building where John Jaques made the Hudson Valley's first commercial wine in 1839. Jaques' interest in grapes was likely inspired by the Croton Point vineyards; the bricks for his cellar came from the Underhill's Croton Point brickyard. (*Courtesy of Brotherhood Wine Co.*)

business had eroded badly. The cellar inventory dated back 35 years. The Emersons had been buying bulk wine from Jaques, blending it with wine from another Hudson Valley producer, the so-called Brotherhood of the New Life, and selling it under a "Brotherhood" label, a name that seemed to bridge the sacramental and secular markets. The new owners renamed their operation The Brotherhood Wine Company and immediately began digging more cellars, adding additions and a cross-vault to the original winery. In their hands it grew rapidly into a Hudson Valley institution; within ten years the vineyards contained 68 grape varieties producing 25,000 gallons of sacramental and table wines and brandy, in cavernous new cellars.

The Brotherhood of the New Life contributes a brief, eccentric footnote to the Hudson Valley story. The Brotherhood was a commune of families settled for a few years near the village of Amenia, in the Taconic foothills of the Hudson region. They were led by the charismatic Christian mystic Thomas Lake Harris, whose flock included

English aristocrats and Japanese samurai; Horace Greeley was briefly an admirer. Harris mesmerized them with poetic, trance-induced recitations that sometimes unfurled for hours. His community supported itself by making wine Harris declared to be divinely infused with "the finer electro-vinous spirit of the collective body of the grape." It was sold in the mid-1860s through the Emerson merchant firm, blended with wine from John Jaques, eventually attaching the Brotherhood label to the wines made in Washingtonville.

In the hamlet of Hardenburgh, west of Washingtonville, Charles A. Hulse had been making wine singled out for high praise in New York City circles since the 1850s. Hulse knew John Jaques well; they were both elders in the Washingtonville Presbyterian Church. Hulse's wines were mentioned regularly in *Cozzens Wine Press*, the newsletter of a prominent New York wine merchant dealing in the most prestigious French chateaux and Champagnes but at the same time ardently promoting fledgling American wineries. Frederick Cozzens introduced New York to the Ohio Valley wines of Nicholas Longworth—the most celebrated winemaker in America—often headlining the newsletter with twin pitches for Longworth and for Hulse's "delicate sweet wines . . . not to be surpassed by the most luscious products of Europe." Cozzens was a salesman dealing in hyperbole but he seemed genuinely thrilled to witness the birth of a new wine region: "grape culture will soon prove to be one of the most valuable fields for enterprise ever presented to the people of the state of New York . . . and the day may not be far off when ships shall lay beside the rich vineyards on the Hudson's banks, to receive the golden fraughtage for distant Europe."

In Columbia County, the Shaker community at New Lebanon included vineyards in their progressive farming enterprise. They grew Concord and tried the Muscadine grape, a southern variety, for sale as fresh fruit and for their own commercial wine label.

Vineyards never did engulf the river in the manner of the German Rhine, but they parried with orchards for possession of a stretch of the Hudson's western shore in Ulster County between Newburgh and Kingston. The most impressive example was the estate of Robert L. Pell, scion of one of New York's old English baronial families. Alongside his huge orchards Pell planted 50 acres of Isabella grapes

FIGURE 2.3. When the last son of John Jaques died in 1885, the business was taken over by its longtime distributors, Jesse and Edward Emerson. They renamed it the Brotherhood Wine Company after their signature label, and immediately started digging cross-vaulted cellars for this imposing, Dutch-influenced, step-gabled winery. (*Courtesy of Kroch Library, Cornell University*)

in the 1850s, encouraged by Richard Underhill's beachhead in the New York City market. During harvest Pelham Farm dispatched four steamboat-loads of fruit every day from its private docks in Esopus to the city and on to Europe, as Cozzens envisioned. But none of it went to wine. For farmers, the quick, cheap shipment of produce to urban markets too easily trumped any interest in local wine.

A neighbor of Pell's, the naturalist John Burroughs, planted and tended a vineyard of Delaware and Niagara for many years at the river's edge near West Park. He wrote many of his essays, as he described in the preface to his collection *Leaf and Tendril*, "in a little bark-covered study that is surrounded on all sides by vineyards." They provided both a working sanctuary and a little extra income for a pastoral writer. He called his nine acres of grapes Riverby, also the title of his last book. Locals called him not the famous man of letters but "the vine-dresser of Esopus."

Within the growing number of Hudson Valley grape farmers there evolved a lively community of grapevine breeders, dating back to the Prince family's work in Flushing. For decades, as they tested European varieties and chance hybrids like Isabella and Catawba, the Princes also attempted to create their own Euro-American hybrids. Like most of the breeders to come, they were ardent wine lovers as well as practical nurserymen, keen to develop grapes good for both eating fresh and for wine. Of the 10,000 seedlings growing at the Linnaean gardens in the 1830s, many were deliberate crosses made from a collection of species and varieties unequaled in the country. But the Princes never chose to commercially release a hybrid grape of their own design.

Crossing grapevine species and varieties was a gambling game; one might play for decades and never win, or roll the lucky combination early on. A neighbor of the Princes in Flushing, Dr. William Valk, carried on experiments breeding grapevines at his own backyard nursery and after just seven years of trials, in 1852, he presented a new variety to the American Pomological Society. Named Ada, it was the first *deliberate* hybrid of European vinifera and native American parentage to be listed by the society and enter commercial circulation, the result of meticulously dusting the pistil of an Isabella flower with the pollen of a European Black Hamburgh, then propagating their seed. Ada never claimed much acreage but it marked the beginning of an almost frenzied period of grape breeding and propagation, by amateurs and professional nurserymen from Massachusetts to Kansas, nowhere quite so intensively as in the Hudson Valley.

The river town of Newburgh was a center of horticultural enterprise, the home of Charles and Andrew Jackson Downing, J. H. Ricketts, William Curlburt, A. J. Caywood, and C. W. Grant. A Newburgh dentist, Grant purchased a 119-acre island nearby in the Hudson to pursue his avocation with grapes. Like Croton Point, Iona Island bathed in the beneficent weather carried upriver by the tides, and Grant's little vineyard swelled into the largest fruit nursery of its day, with 30 greenhouses. He sold grapes to New York City and Albany and vines throughout the East. In 1863 he introduced, with great fanfare, a new grape variety he named Iona, a second-generation seedling of Catawba advertised as "unequalled for fine, rich, enduring wine . . . It is only with such grapes as this that we can equal the fine wines of Europe." Iona was an immediate commercial and critical success. When *New York Herald American* editor Horace Greeley announced an award for the best new American grape variety, it went to Iona.

The new grape's superior wine quality was indisputable, but its finicky performance in the vineyard soon knocked it off its pedestal; on anything but the best sites it tended to give miserly crops of thin fruit. Bombarded with criticism from the field, Grant returned his prize, which then went to a new variety from Concord, Massachusetts, proclaimed by Greeley "the grape for the millions." The humiliated Grant soon closed his business and abandoned his island vineyards. The Iona grape, however, carried on, a favorite of growers establishing vineyards on the Finger Lakes, where it became an agent of finesse in sparkling wine cuvees.

Grant's colleague Andrew J. Caywood set his vineyard on a steep slope above the village of Marlborough. He had been drawn to viticulture as a young man by his brother-in-law William Cornell, who planted one of Ulster County's first vineyards near Clintondale in 1845. Cornell was in turn the brother-in-law of William Underhill and his vines came from the Underhills' Croton Point, as viticulture climbed up the Hudson Valley through family ties. Caywood began hybridizing grapes when he was in his twenties and stuck with it for nearly 50 years, turning out several named varieties. One of them, Dutchess, introduced around 1880, became another favorite in the Finger Lakes.

During the last half of the nineteenth century, around 2,000 hybrid grape varieties were named and disseminated in America; the press called it "grape mania." A disproportionate number of those hybrids came out of Hudson Valley nurseries. Local growers were particularly susceptible to the smorgasbord of choices laid out before them with breathless descriptions. Vineyards planted around the valley typically included a mix of many new releases; the valley served as a massive research center.

This was not necessarily a formula for commercial success. To try out a new carrot took an investment of one season; a new grape required four or five years. In time almost all the 2,000 new grape varieties failed the tests of disease or winter-kill or a fickle market.

As vines struggled and disappointed, new vineyards were left ragged, under-productive, and uneconomical. Vineyard acreage in the Hudson Valley peaked by 1890 when the U.S. Census of Agriculture reported 13,000 acres. In the next census at the turn of the century, the valley's acreage dropped by more than half; the locus of commercial viticulture had shifted west to the Finger Lakes and Great Lakes. It was even more true for wine. When U. P. Hedrick wrote his landmark reference, *The Grapes of New York*, in 1908, he noted that the valley had only two or three wineries, using a mere 5 percent of its grapes.

One of those wineries, however, was just getting started, the enterprise of banker Alessandro Bolognesi and his large, Italian-immigrant family. Along bluffs across the Hudson from Poughkeepsie, the Bolognesis built a fieldstone winery compound with its own campanile—an ode to their Tuscan roots—surrounded by 350 rolling acres of vines. Their wines gained the reputation of bright stars in a troubled sky.

CHAPTER 3

Settling in the Finger Lakes

How soon land suitable for grape growing ran up from 25 to 500 dollars per acre; even good farmers who were doing well on their farms must have a vineyard—doctors, lawyers, merchants, clergymen, mechanics, in fact a perfect stampede among every class to get a vineyard.

A few years after French explorer Samuel de Champlain's first probe into the New York wilderness, on the lake that would later bear his name, he set out with a band of Huron Indians on a raid into the lake-country homeland of the Haudenosaunee. The French called the lake-country Indians "Iroquois"—clowns—for the way they painted their faces. Champlain's party canoed up the St. Lawrence River from Quebec, crossed Lake Ontario, and struck inland toward the Finger Lakes in the summer of 1615. In his journal he wrote "vines and nuts are in great quantities, and grapes come to maturity there, but they leave always a sharp, sour taste, which proceeds from want of cultivation; but those that have been cultivated in these parts are of pretty good flavor."

Cultivated Iroquois vineyards? Not likely, but Champlain must have seen some attempt to domesticate ambient grapevines lurking on the edge of woods alongside Indian gardens. There were precedents. Fifty years earlier the French cartographer-artist Jacques LeMoyne, on an exploration of the Atlantic coast, sketched an Indian village with grapevines in open-ground semi-cultivation. We know from early Dutch observations that Native Americans pressed wild grapes for juice. We are left to wonder how, by all first-contact accounts, they did not know wine, what juice so naturally becomes.

Where French explorers led, Jesuit Catholic missionaries soon followed. Father Simon LeMoyne led the first mission to the Iroquois in 1654, on Onondaga Lake. Within ten years there were missions to all five Indian nations. The Jesuit fathers regularly reported back to the church hierarchy in Europe, their letters later published as *The Jesuit Relations*, describing Indian society in great detail and the missionary determination to infuse it with Christianity.

In a letter from the Mission of St. Francis Xavier dated 1668, Father Jacques Bruyas wrote,

> This place is fairly pleasant, although it has none of the features which give beauty to our country homes. If one were to take the trouble to plant some vines and trees, they would yield as well as they do in France; but the savage is too fond of wandering to be made to cultivate them. Nevertheless, apple, plum, and chestnut trees are seen here; but all these fruits are of little importance, and do not have the same taste as those of France . . . There are also vines, which bear tolerably good grapes, from which our fathers formerly made wine for the mass. I believe that, if they were pruned two years in succession, the grapes would be as good as those of France.

By this account, mid-seventeenth-century French missionaries made the first Finger Lakes wine, perhaps the first in New York, to serve at Mass for "the savages."

By the late 1600s the Jesuit missions had become casualties of the conflict between France and England for control of New York. By the late 1700s that conflict, hardly missing a drumbeat, had shifted into one between England and the American colonies.

At the height of the American Revolution, George Washington sent one-third of his Army of the Continental Congress into the land of the Iroquois. Most of the Six Nations had allied with the British, periodically raiding colonial settlements and military outposts in the Mohawk and Susquehanna Valleys. In September 1779, to put an end to Indian harassment, Washington directed Generals William Sullivan and James Clinton to sack the Seneca and Cayuga Iroquois homeland. For three weeks, more than 4,000 soldiers combed the western Finger Lakes region, encountering little resistance, burning villages and crops. Roadside historical signs put up 200 years later trace their route up and down and between the lakes.

Journals from soldiers in the Sullivan-Clinton expedition noted a profusion of grapevines along their march, not surprisingly; wild grapes were a common sight snaking through the trees of eastern America. What did astonish soldiers was the sight of huge orchards of apple and peach. At one Cayuga village they cut down 1,500 peach trees, some of them more than a century old, planted from seeds or cuttings brought by Jesuit missionaries. The culture of peaches was unknown so far north, but they had flourished in islands of warmth created by the lakes, foretelling a ripe future for Finger Lakes viticulture: where peaches grew, even the tenderest grapes might find a home.

The land around the lakes was an almost unbroken, rolling forest of oak, chestnut, ash, walnut, and maple, webbed with footpaths under towering canopies. All but a few overlooked Indian villages had been destroyed. With no food or shelter through the winter of 1779–80, most of the Iroquois fled to the Niagara region for British protection, but some lingered or drifted back after the war. They were outsiders in their own homeland as the first white settlers trickled into Indian clearings in the years around 1790, building log houses and planting homestead gardens that incorporated the odd surviving fruit tree. One of those clearings, at the head of Keuka Lake, grew into the hamlet of Hammondsport.

Most of the lakes dissolved into marshlands at their southern ends but the land at the head of Keuka was firm enough to support settlement directly on the water. The early settlers called Keuka "Crooked Lake" after its slingshot shape. A cluster of cabins and mills grew up by the 1820s and at the end of that decade Richard Sheffield arrived from the Hudson Valley to open the village's first tavern. He brought with him a few cuttings of two grape varieties from the Linnaean Nursery on Long Island: Isabella and Catawba.

After a tavern the village needed next a church. In 1829 a young Reverend William Bostwick, fresh out of seminary in Connecticut, arrived in Hammondsport to establish the town's first Episcopal Church. He knew the area; he'd been one of the first graduates of Hobart College in Geneva.

In this backcountry Bostwick lacked a source of sacramental wine. With trimmings from Sheffield's vines, he planted grapevines in his rectory garden, they flourished, and like the Jesuits before him, he made his own church wine. This was no chore for him. He was an avid amateur horticulturist, an occasional contributor to the local *Genesee Valley Farmer & Gardener's Journal*, with a secular appreciation for wine and a visionary interest in hybridization. "Our native grapes, embracing several species and many varieties, have some excellent properties which the foreign grape does not possess," he wrote in the Genesee journal, "the hardy texture of its wood, which adapts it to our varied climate, and the luxuriance of its growth. On the other hand, the European grape possesses a decided advantage in the thinness of its skin, the absence of pulp, and the richness of its juices. By crossing them, and producing hybrids, we propose to combine the excellencies of both." At the time, grape breeding was just beginning to engage a few horticultural pioneers. Bostwick probably never attempted any crossings, but he was soon giving away or selling Catawba and Isabella vines to his parishioners.

Grapes began decorating arbors around town, then filling out small gardens and yards. One of Bostwick's viticultural apostles was William Hastings, the operator of Hammondsport's first general store and a leading citizen of the hamlet. He planted his vines in a terraced garden on the edge of town where all could see how well they grew. The garden plot multiplied into Hammondsport's first little vineyard and, in 1847, Hastings arranged a shipment of 50 pounds of grapes and a quantity of jelly by Erie Canal to New York City. The proceeds barely covered his cost of shipping. He also made wine in the large cellar of his home, and sent some through Bostwick's church to the Episcopal Diocese of Western New York, where it earned the bishop's imprimatur.

Another member of Bostwick's congregation and an admirer of Hastings' vineyard, Josiah W. Prentiss, put vines in several miles up

FIGURE 3.1. The missionary of Finger Lakes wine Rev. William Bostwick, rector of Hammondsport's first church. He was not the first to plant wine grapes in the Lake District or western New York, but his dissemination of vine cuttings to church parishioners in the early 1830s, and his promotion of winemaking, seeded the Finger Lakes wine district. (*Courtesy of Richard Murphy and St. Thomas' Episcopal Church, Bath*)

the west side of Keuka Lake at Pulteney, around 1838. He planted his first cuttings at a summer house in the hills too far back, as it turned out, from the lake. Earlier-ripening Isabella fared better than Catawba—first lessons in the demands of different varieties and the climatic reach of the lake.

Prentiss threw himself into this new line of farming with more enthusiasm than knowledge but with intelligence and the practical savvy of a trailblazer. He took cuttings from his summer-house vines to start a new vineyard hugging the lake at a settlement called Harmonyville. There he staked his vines to trellis posts nine feet high and let the trunks run up to the top and spill over like fountains in rows 14 feet apart. The vineyard grew to three acres by the early 1850s, generating regular shipments of fresh grapes to the nearby village of Bath. In 1854 Prentiss sent the first large shipment of grapes—two tons of Isabellas—to New York City by steamboat, wagon, and a new railhead at Bath. Richard Underhill's Croton Point vineyard had recently opened the big-city market for table grapes and the railroad suddenly made it more accessible. Prentiss's Isabellas brought him a sensational 16 cents a pound—$320 per ton. He also started making small amounts of wine, sold locally, informally, to churches and pharmacies.

Josiah Prentiss's vineyard caught the attention of a young German immigrant, Andrew Reisinger, a cooper raised in wine country on the Rhine. When he saw what Prentiss had accomplished riding herd on what may have looked to him more like an orchard than a vineyard, Reisinger saw a future in the Finger Lakes. In 1852 he struck a deal with Prentiss's neighbor in Harmonyville, Melchior Wagener: Reisinger would plant and tend two or three acres with German expertise, Wagener would supply the land and pay for vines; profits to be shared.

Andrew Reisinger traveled to Cincinnati to purchase 4,000 Catawba cuttings from Nicholas Longworth, then America's leading winegrower. For vineyard rows at the Harmonyville site, trenches were dug three feet deep, refilled partly with a bed of stones and bones, then with compost and topsoil, and finally terraced to the water's edge. Vines were densely planted, four feet apart in rows only four feet wide, and trained low to a trellis only four feet high to capture ground heat—all in the German way. Trunks were renewed from the ground annually. In its second year bearing fruit, the vineyard produced three tons to the acre, three times what Prentiss and others were getting.

Prentiss himself declared Reisinger's Harmonyville vineyard "the first scientific effort at grape growing, for wine, in the Crooked Lake district . . . When grape growing first commenced as a business in Pulteney, many came to me to learn how to grow grapes. What little I knew was learned by experience, and was easy told. But when Mr. Reisinger stepped on deck, I had to retire to the hold."

With their growing habits distinct from the European grapevines he knew, the native varieties didn't always bend to Reisinger's regimen; there were plenty of lessons to be learned. And Prentiss did not stay down in the hold. When rot appeared on Reisinger's grapes, more than Prentiss had seen on his own, he came up and blamed it on too-intensive cultivation, too much Teutonic discipline: "Proper cultivation and training can do much to promote the growth and increase the fruit, but like everything else it can be overdone . . . we cannot carry out these diversions too far from nature's law with impunity." The lessons were only just beginning. Rot and other vine diseases would come, inexorably, to Prentiss's vineyard as well, with heavier crop loads and the monoculture of more extensive plantings. Historian W. Woodward Clayton, writing 25 years later in his *History of Steuben County*, characterized Reisinger's effort as "rather a failure," but if so, it was a failure that opened doors and minds, and at the time it was deemed a breakthrough to European standards.

Among the inspired, two prominent figures in the Hammondsport community—Judge Jacob Larrowe and his neighbor Orlando Shepard—hired Reisinger in 1855 to establish the first commercial vineyards on the slopes along Pleasant Valley, the dry, topographical echo of Keuka Lake running south from Hammondsport. The planting material came from vineyards in Livingston County west of the Finger Lakes (more on them in the next chapter). They were only half-an-acre each, but the sight of Larrowe's and Shepard's vineyards hovering above Hammondsport touched off a flurry of new plantings along the valley.

With his innovations on Keuka Lake duly noted, Andrew Reisinger moved on—to the next lake west, Canandaigua, where he could now afford his own place.

To the valley at the south end of Canandaigua Lake, akin to Keuka's Pleasant Valley, an attorney in the village of Naples named James Monier brought what may well have been the first cultivated grapevines to the Finger Lakes, a couple of Isabella and Catawba vines from Long Island, probably from the Linnaean Nursery. This was several years before the same grapes arrived in Hammondsport. Monier's garden vines were in full display 20 years later when fellow lawyer Edward McKay took notice and studied whatever agronomic research he could find to determine if grape growing was a good commercial bet for Naples. He then did some nineteenth-century backcountry market research of his own: he bought a bushel of Monier's grapes, boxed them up and took them on a 100-mile buggy ride around western New York to see, he later wrote, "whether the grape would bear carrying to market . . . and when taken out of the box they were in perfect condition."

McKay took cuttings from Monier to test in his own garden and a few years later set out the town's first vineyard—160 Isabella vines—in 1847. A fellow townsman described McKay preparing his vineyard in "an unusual and unnecessary way. It so happened that a number of cattle were being pastured nearby, a number of them died, and Mr. McKay getting possession of them, buried portions of them at intervals of 16 feet apart, in the row, the rows being 16 feet apart . . . His first acre produced an enormous crop of grapes the fourth year."

McKay took this first crop to Montreal by wagon and canal. He also took his grapes to the railhead at Bath, competing with a disgruntled Josiah Prentiss: ". . . soon McKay of Naples came down with his fancy boxes, and raised the price to ten cents a pound . . . the Naples people know how he 'pushed things,' or rather his wife did." First deliveries of Canandaigua and Keuka grapes had arrived in Montreal and New York City at about the same time.

When Andrew Reisinger saw Edward McKay's vineyard in Naples he was again impressed by the accomplishment of an amateur. He bought land for a vineyard of his own not far from McKay. A year later another German vine-dresser, Philip Dinzler, settled on the same hillside west of town, initiating a parade of German immigrants (and at least two German-speaking Swiss) through the coming decades. They turned Naples and the southern end of Canandaigua Lake into the second early hub of Finger Lakes viticulture.

The first tentative steps toward winemaking around the Finger Lakes, as in other nascent American vineyard districts, had come through the church. Temperance sentiment kept a lid, or attempted to, on ventures into the commercial wine market. The Reverend Bostwick was himself a controversial figure in Hammondsport, preaching the gospel while distributing what some townsfolk held to be the seeds of debauchery. He encouraged his grape-growing disciples to experiment with winemaking as he had done, and not just for sacramental use. When he left Hammondsport for missionary work in Illinois in 1843, someone stole into the rectory garden and ripped out his vines.

The decade of the 1850s brought the first legislative sorties of the prohibition movement around the nation: scattered state and local laws restricted the production or sale of alcohol in various ways. New York dabbled in these legal efforts only briefly. As the decade ended, grape-growing was also blooming, spreading up both sides of Keuka Lake to Penn Yan and the bluff between Keuka's two arms; also along the western slope of Naples Valley and around the southern end of Canandaigua Lake at Middlesex and Vine Valleys. The slopes along the lakeshores had been the first land cleared of trees when early settlers laid low the Finger Lakes' magnificent hardwood forest for lumber. These side hills were too steep for field crops. They were looked upon as virtually worthless real estate until grapes came along, terraced—as Reisinger had demonstrated—to hug the ripening warmth of the water. The *Hammondsport Herald* marveled at "How soon land suitable for grape growing ran up from 25 to 500 dollars per acre; even good farmers who were doing well on their farms must have a vineyard—doctors, lawyers, merchants, clergymen, mechanics, in fact a perfect stampede among every class to get a vineyard."

Virtually all the grapes grown were sold as fresh fruit, but the market for table grapes was still new, kindled by the very appearance of American varieties like Catawba and Isabella with their voluptuous aromas and flavors. The demand for grapes proved not so easy to grow as the grapes themselves. The 16 cents per pound Josiah Prentiss made in 1854 dropped to 6 cents within a few years as more grapes flooded the infant market.

Vineyards were still small, typically not more than a few acres, but more numerous year by year. In 1858 one Pleasant Valley grower made a buying trip to Kelley's Island, Ohio—at that time one of the nation's major vineyard districts—and brought back 30,000 grapevine cuttings, a huge infusion of planting material for his own property and half a dozen neighbors. That collegial group formed the area's first farming collective, the Pleasant Valley Grape Growers Association. They had a reputation described by one observer as "a class of well-to-do farmers who were remarkably liberal in their habits and opinions. Not particularly choice in their moral propriety. . . ." The scent of wine was in the air.

In 1857, the enterprising Josiah Prentiss made what appears to have been the Finger Lake's first seriously marketed commercial vintage: "Highland Cottage" Isabella and Catawba, with florid labels designed by the winemaker himself (he was an accomplished landscape and portrait painter). There is no record of quantity. Highland Cottage had a broker in New York City, but it was a modest effort, and short-lived. Within a few years the label disappeared and Prentiss turned his attention back to his vineyard.

About the same time Josiah Prentiss made his move, Pleasant Valley grower Grattan Wheeler founded Wheeler's Hammondsport Wine Company at his four-acre vineyard. But Wheeler had only just planted his vines and it is unclear when his company actually started making wine.

Other adventurous souls were learning what to do with a glut of grapes. The Union Horticultural Society of Penn Yan reported, in 1859: "[T]here have been not less than 1,636 gallons of wine made in this vicinity . . . from nearly all our varieties of grapes, with varying success, as may be expected when inexperienced men engage in a new enterprise. The business is extending, and is destined to become important."

At the head of Cayuga Lake, according to Ithaca physician S. J. Parker, "[t]he vintage of this town, in 1858, was about 1,000 gallons, of which over 600 were made by my press." He had been making wine for 15 years, a doggedly practical blend of under-ripe Catawba ("usually ripens poorly") with ripe Isabella. "We probably have in town over 600 gallons ripe and for sale. With unreasonable suspicion we can find no ready sale, but in time this will be overcome."

All these earnest, stumbling, individual initiatives cried out for a collective effort pooling the resources needed—creative, financial, agricultural—to offer a new economic model for the Finger Lakes. That breakthrough came in 1860 when Grattan Wheeler, perhaps frustrated by the challenges of his own Hammondsport Wine Company, threw his lot in with a group of Pleasant Valley grape growers to form the Hammondsport and Pleasant Valley Wine Company. Thirteen investors accounted for a total of 200 shares at $50 per share. One of the larger growers, Aaron Baker, had brought the 30,000 vine cuttings to the valley from Ohio only a couple of years earlier. The smallest grower with just one acre of vines, Charles Champlin, was a major investor and guiding force. His little vineyard climbed the slope behind property he deeded to the company for construction of a wine cellar. Wheeler became the new company's president; Champlin its secretary-treasurer. They hired John Weber, German born and trained, as winemaker.

Weber had recently visited the area as an agent of the U. S. Patent Office's agricultural branch, on an extended field study of grape culture through the northeast states, collecting vine specimens and assessing

FIGURE 3.2. The Pleasant Valley Wine Company, the Finger Lakes' first successful winery, was the collective venture of 13 grape-growing stockholders, some of them here holding court on the portico of their new building. Prime-mover Charles D. Champlin stands second from the right. A temperance-minded townsperson described the group as "a class of well-to-do farmers who were remarkably liberal in their habits and opinions. Not particularly choice in their moral propriety." (*Courtesy of Pleasant Valley Wine Co.*)

the potential for a regional wine industry. His report, published by the patent office in 1859, radiated optimism and laid out practical guidelines for grape growers and winemakers. The Finger Lakes, in particular, looked to him like Germany with hardly any vines. A year later he had quit the patent office, was supervising the first vintage at Pleasant Valley, and preparing to plant his own vineyard on the hillside west of Hammondsport. The company's 1860 production of the stalwarts Isabella and Catawba totaled 4,200 gallons pressed from 20 tons of grapes, one of which came up the lake from the vineyard of Josiah Prentiss. By now there were hundreds of acres of bearing vineyards to draw from and hundreds more planted. Finger Lakes wine had arrived.

Even as grape growers settled down to the business of making wine with American grape varieties, the dream of making American wine from European vinifera vines—stymied again and again for 200 years—refused to fade. The new Pleasant Valley Wine Company sales catalogue included this declaration:

> Contrary to all experience in other places, the best varieties of European wine grapes have continued to do well here, and bear fair quantities of the finest of fruit. In spite of all opposition some of our most enterprising German vine-dressers have persisted in putting out quite large vineyards of the best Foreign grapes, importing the roots and cuttings directly from home for that purpose. These vines, with moderate protection in winter, have continued to thrive and do well, ripening a fair amount of fruit last season . . . some retained and manufactured into wine . . . and the new wine is of very fine quality, commanding higher prices than that from any of our American grapes.

Quantities, varieties, how the wines were sold and other details were not mentioned, and the next paragraph tacked on the fateful caveat "of course we may fail, all experience in this country being against us." And indeed they did fail. But for a few years, at least, vinifera vines were grown around Hammondsport by German vine-dressers, likely including John Weber, and at least some wine came from them in vintage 1862. The Pleasant Valley company showed an exhibit of grapes in October of that year at the State Fair in Rochester, where one member of the wine committee admired "numerous French and German varieties of wine grape cultivated by them with perfect success thus far, indicating no signs of rust or mildew."

The same Pleasant Valley catalogue advertised 42 varieties of grapevines for sale from the winery's experimental nursery, 15 of them "foreign varieties" including Riesling, Traminer, and Burgundy, the American name for Pinot Noir. The foreigners disappeared in future catalogues.

The activity around Hammondsport encouraged more planting at Naples and Canandaigua Lake, propelled by an influx of German immigrants. The leading banker in town, German-born Hiram Maxfield, began buying vineyards in 1858 and, a year after the Pleasant Valley Wine Co. opened, he nested a hexagonal stone cellar into a slope of vines on the edge of Naples for the Canandaigua Lake region's first winery. Andrew Reisinger's nearby vineyard must have been a key supplier. With a banker's resources, Maxfield's Naples Valley Wine Company had a solid start but on a more cautious scale than the cellar at Pleasant Valley.

These wineries appeared on the eve of the Civil War. The drain that conflict put on the local economy and its workforce slowed the development of winegrowing in the Finger Lakes as elsewhere. Fewer vineyards went in during the war years 1861–65 and only one small winery opened, the Freidell Wine Company. Mathias Freidell had arrived in Hammondsport from Germany in 1858. He bought the elegant home of William Hastings and expanded its terraced garden of vines to a six-acre vineyard. In the house's large cellar, where Hastings had made small batches of sacramental wine two decades earlier, Freidell produced his first vintage in 1863. His little winery would be one of the region's most enduring.

After the war winegrowing resumed with pent-up energy. More grape varieties appeared on the grower's and the winemaker's palette. Delaware and Concord were spreading rapidly through the region, beginning to displace Isabella (though not Catawba). A cascade of new varieties filled the pages of nursery catalogues—Diana, Clinton, Iona, Ives, Eumelan, Israella, Salem, Walter, Norton, Crevelling—seducing farmers with extravagant claims and testimonials.

There was genuine excitement on Keuka with the opening of Urbana Wine Company in 1865, capitalized at a quarter of a million dollars, the region's most ambitious new enterprise of its day. Growers Clark Bell and Guy McMaster, with 225 acres in vines along the lake north of Hammondsport, joined a half dozen other investors to excavate what newspaper accounts called the largest wine cellar in the United States, capped with a magnificent, 150-foot long, four-

FIGURE 3.3. A sparkling wine finishing line at the Urbana Wine Company. At back right, bottles have arrived from aging/riddling racks and disgorged their sediment from secondary fermentation in the bottle (note the wet floor). Urbana's French champagne-maker Charles LeBreton is credited with inventing the process of freezing the sediment into a plug that minimized spilled wine. As they pass up the line, bottles are topped-up (dosaged), corked (by the man with the pull ring), wired, capsuled, wrapped in paper, nested in straw, and nailed into wooden boxes—all with manual power, no electricity. (*Courtesy of the Fred and Harriet Taylor Memorial Library*)

story stone factory. The cellar's arched ceiling ran 18 feet high. The roof sprouted a row of steeples; it was a temple of wine. The company itself cut a road into the cliffs along the lake shore for four miles to connect the winery directly with Hammondsport.

Bell and McMaster were also among the original investors in the Pleasant Valley Wine Company. Along with Grattan Wheeler they were initiating a new class of diversified, Keuka Lake wine entrepreneurs. They hired Charles LeBreton from the celebrated Louis Roederer Champagne house in Rheims, France, to design and run a facility explicitly for the production of sparkling wine. Located directly on Keuka's shore, the new winery had its own steamboat landing linked to the Erie Canal, giving Urbana an uninterrupted water route to distant markets. The landing also touched off a planting spree of hundreds more vineyard acres on the lake's opposite shore, where growers could easily deliver their grapes by boat. By the time Urbana opened, the press-house tally at Pleasant Valley had risen ten-fold to 200 tons but it was soon eclipsed by Urbana. The rivalry between Pleasant Valley and Urbana would energize both wineries and the entire Keuka Lake winegrowing scene for many years.

In the same year Urbana hired LeBreton, the Pleasant Valley winery hired another French Champagne-maker originally from Rheims but via Ohio, Joseph Masson. He was soon joined by his brother Jules when his job supervising the Longworth Wine House disappeared with the collapse of that venerable Cincinnati operation. Nicholas Longworth had created America's first bona-fide vineyard district and its first prosperous wine business, starting in the 1830s on the Ohio River. Its precipitous decline three decades later, from vineyards overrun with black rot and mildew, came just as Finger Lakes wineries burst on the scene, releasing a migration of winemaking talent from Ohio to New York.

With that migration came the specialized art of champagne. Longworth and his fellow Ohio Valley winemakers had learned to exploit a natural affinity of native grapes—with their relatively low sugar levels and high acidity—for making sparkling wine. These were ripening parameters familiar in the cool northern Champagne district of France. The vibrant flavors of American grapes also tended to calm down in the aging process for sparkling wine, and resonate with effervescence, as in Longworth's wildly successful Sparkling Catawba.

Until 1865, European expertise imported to the Finger Lakes had come almost exclusively from Germany, a vignette within the wave of German emigration to the United States in the early mid-nineteenth century. Pleasant Valley's first winemaker John (Johann) Weber made only still wine and brandy (his plans for PV's distillery were drawn up in German). The same was true of Hiram Maxfield and Mathias Freidell. The introduction of sparkling wine came with the arrival of French Champenois—from Ohio and from France—after the Civil War. They soon dominated Keuka Lake winemaking while German immigrants made still wine in Naples Valley.

Marshall P. Wilder, president of the American Pomological Society and the nation's preeminent horticulturist, presided at a meeting of the Pleasant Valley Grape Growers Association in 1870 to assess new grape varieties and wines. At the meeting Charles Champlin unveiled samples of Pleasant Valley Wine's new sparkling blend, the handiwork of Jules Masson and the first to include Delaware grapes in the cuvee. Wilder

FIGURE 3.4. The village of Hammondsport, circa 1870, with vines cascading down Bully Hill in the foreground, more vineyards climbing the ridge to the east, and Pleasant Valley trailing off between. Steamboats carried wine in barrels from new wineries to the Erie Canal connection at the lake's north end. (*Courtesy of the Fred and Harriet Taylor Memorial Library*)

reportedly declared it "the great champagne of the West . . . you might appropriate the Western Continent to yourself. . . ." PV's marketing team was listening: "Great Western Champagne" appeared on the label of the next vintage. Two years later that wine earned a gold medal at the Vienna World Exposition, a stunning accolade from European judges for an American-grape wine. Great Western would become, for decades, the most famous sparkling wine in America.

As PV's production swelled, shipping became an issue. The nearest steamboat landing was a mile away; a costly interruption in the water route to market by canal. The closest railroad, in Bath, was nine wagon-miles away. Lurching wagons made a bad match with sparkling wine. In the early 1870s the winery partnered with town officials and steamboat operators to finance construction of a Bath & Hammondsport Rail Road. "Not as long as the others," the B&H slogan winked, "but just as wide."

Wide enough to carry both wine and fresh grapes on a new transportation channel dramatically faster than the route to market by lake and canal. And unexpectedly, the B&H began bringing back into Hammondsport an influx of tourists. The post-Civil War age of railroads and the new national pastime of tourism had arrived at the doorstep of Finger Lakes wine. Railroad companies immediately began offering excursion packages to New York's lake country from Buffalo, Philadelphia, New York City and beyond. Steamboat companies added more boats linking the Hammondsport depot with hotels and winery landings. Wineries responded with tours and tastings. A flyer for the queen of hotels on Keuka Lake, the Grove Springs House, described its location "in the heart of the Grape and Wine districts with immense wineries . . . millions of bottles of champagne . . . A trip through any one of the cellars is very interesting and visitors always welcome."

The Steuben County seat of Bath, one of the Finger Lakes' original settlement towns, now lay at the junction of a railroad to vineyards and a railroad to major urban markets. A cluster of wineries sprouted around Bath's depot—the Seeley Wine Company, McCormick Wine Company, Steuben County Vineyard Association, Bath Wine Company. A few vineyards dotted the hills around town but Bath was too far from the lake to be good grape land. These were railroad wineries, bringing fruit in and shipping wine out all by train.

With new transportation connections, a wave of tourism, an infusion of French winemaking talent to Keuka Lake and German talent to Canandaigua—Finger Lakes wine was hitting its stride. Much of Keuka's shoreline was now blanketed with vineyards. Grapes were spilling over to Seneca Lake. Planting on Seneca had started by 1845 when James Vescelius put in propagation vines for nurseryman Isaac Hildreth on his farm in Eddytown (later renamed Lakemont). The first sizeable vineyard was probably J. S. Easely's five acres on the lake's shore near the Glenora Point steamboat landing in 1859. He added another five acres the following year.

James Valentine planted a small Seneca vineyard at Severne Point below Himrod in 1862. After the war the Seneca Lake Grape Wine Company formed around the nucleus of Valentine's vineyard, expanding it rapidly to 150 acres; newspapers called it the biggest single block of grapevines in the state. It was meticulously laid out by the son of Pleasant Valley vineyard pioneer Jacob Larrowe, following the design Andrew Reisinger had used for Larrowe's vineyard 10 years earlier, but by this time wire trellis had replaced cumbersome mazes of wooden-lath crossbars.

The Seneca Company's four-and-a-half-story stone winery went up on benchland above its own steamboat landing at Severne Point. From the uphill side a light-rail track trestled to an upper floor, carrying grapes above high-arched cellars to a sorting room where perfect fruit was packed for the fresh market and culls went to the press. The cellar had a storage capacity of 250,000 gallons. In its debut vintage, 1870, the winery produced 14,000 gallons of Seneca Lake's first wine.

The Finger Lakes wine district was also stretching west, to the far side of Hemlock Lake. The first Catholic bishop of Rochester, Bernard McQuaid, bought land on the lake in 1865 for a summer residence and a retreat where his priests could toil in real vineyards. He called the place O-Neh-Da, the Seneca Indian word for the hemlock tree. McQuaid was a cosmopolitan cleric irked by the inferior stuff that passed for wine at communion. The fathers planted a new Worden grape variety, the bishop brought coopers from France to outfit a cellar with first-rate casks, and Rochester-area churches began receiving their altar wines from O-Neh-Da in 1872. "We can retire to the peaceful slopes of Hemlock Lake," McQuaid wrote, "and in the cultivation of the grapes help priests to say Mass with wine that is *wine*."

FIGURE 3.5. The Seneca Lake Wine Company brought winemaking to a third Finger Lake in 1870. The man at right rides a mini-railcar running on a trestle that carried grapes to an upper floor, where perfect fruit was packed for the table market and culls dropped down to the press—a common arrangement in the early wineries. More than a century would pass before Seneca Lake had another winery. (*Courtesy of the Yates County History Center*)

The decades of the 1870s and 80s brought on dozens of new ventures around the lakes. Wineries opening just within the Keuka watershed included Hammondsport Valley Wine Cellars, Haase's Rheims Wine Cellar, Crooked Lake Wine Cellars, Germania Wine Cellars, Connolly Brothers Winery, Lake View Wine Company, McCorn Wine Company, Western New York Wine Company, Pulteney Wine Cellars, Eckel's Wine Cellar, Glen Winery, Crescent Wine Company,

D. Smutz Wine Company, Foster Cellars, Columbia Wine Company, Taylor Wine Company, Monarch Wine Company, Hammondsport Vintage Company, and the Empire State Wine Company.

Some of these ventures conducted business out of farmhouse cellar doors; some were well-capitalized enterprises with regional and national ambitions. The Frey brothers constructed a handsome, Second-Empire stone compound for their Germania winery south of Hammondsport; it presumed to upstage the cellars of the Pleasant Valley Wine Co. next door. Sons of Hammondsport wine pioneer Grattan Wheeler founded the Crooked Lake Wine Company eight miles north of Hammondsport at Gibson's landing, with rambling stone cellars a short hop across the lake from the Grove Springs House. Theirs would become the only winery in the United States dedicated solely to the production of sparkling wine. They lured-away winemaker Charles LeBreton from Urbana to create White Top Champagne, one of New York's star labels in the late 1800s. Urbana then replaced LeBreton with Jules Crance from Moet & Chandon. Finger Lakes wineries were stealing top talent from the *crème de la crème* of French Champagne houses.

In Hammondsport, LaRay McCorn earned a reputation as the most meticulous small-scale winemaker in town. His winery happened to be located across the road from Grimley's Table Grape Packing House, where a young grower on nearby Bully Hill named Walter Taylor brought his fruit for the fresh market. While Taylor waited for his picking lugs to be emptied he liked to hang out with McCorn, listening and observing.

Taylor was a cooper by trade. He had come to Hammondsport in 1879 as a 20-year-old apprentice, bought a small vineyard on the shoulder of Bully Hill, and started selling grapes as a sideline. He was now a cooper with grapes, and the inevitable unfolded with the punctuality of the annual harvest. 1880: he bought a neighbor's 60-acre vineyard and began barreling grape juice as The Taylor Company, one of the first local operations to commercialize the work of Louis Pasteur preserving juice by killing spoilage microorganisms with heat. Taylor made the rounds at railroad stops taking orders for various blends of juice. In 1881 he constructed a three-story press house, outfitting it with his own thousand-gallon oak blending vats. 1882: he had his winery license. Mentored by McCorn and supplied with fortifying

FIGURE 3.6. An 1879 wedding portrait of 21-year-old Walter Taylor and his 19-year-old bride Addie Chapman. He was an apprentice cooper making butter tubs and general-store barrels with his father in Tioga County. Her family had recently moved to Bully Hill, where Walter courted Addie and discovered the world of grapes and wine. A few months after the wedding, a seven-acre vineyard came up for sale next to the Chapmans; the newlyweds bought it, and Walter Taylor was soon making barrels for his Taylor Company. (*Courtesy of the Glenn H. Curtiss Museum*)

brandy by his friends the Frey brothers, he renamed his business the Taylor Wine Company.

In the year Walter Taylor started making wine, a German-speaking Swiss named Johann Jacob Widmer moved his family to Naples, New York, where years earlier his brother had joined the community of immigrants. Widmer had little experience with grapes; he was a master blacksmith who dreamed of designing carriages. A man of possibilities, in a few years he might have entered into the business of horseless carriages, as Glenn Curtiss was experimenting with motorcycles in Hammondsport, but Widmer was drawn instead into the grape rush. He settled his young family on the hillside west of town, where he had only to look over his shoulder at Andrew Reisinger's 30-year-old vineyard for a textbook on his new career. At first "Jake" grew grapes for the fresh fruit market, gradually building up a farm that incorporated a newly released variety named Niagara. He made wine for his own use in his farmhouse cellar until he had honed the skills and stockpiled the inventory to enter the trade in 1888, with two 140-gallon casks of Catawba and Concord, selling wine in kegs and barrels to German immigrants in Rochester.

By this time there were many local colleagues: Philip Dinzler and the Thrall and Rohlin wineries in Naples, Georg Graff on Greisa Hill north of town, the Fox brothers and George Miller wineries on the west shore of Canandaigua Lake, John Seeley in Vine Valley on the east side, Basil Kaltenbach south of town—all of them German family operations. By 1870 there were 800 acres of vines surrounding the village of Naples and in 1876 so many Germans had settled on the road along the west side of town it was renamed Rhine Street. Winemaker Philip Dinzler had a sideline as travel agent, advertising in the *Neopolitan Record* to sell steamer tickets for the trip from Bremen— "purchased here to send to friends in the Old Country."

None of the Naples-Canandaigua family wineries would grow to challenge the dominance of Maxfield Cellars, except Jacob Widmer. His business savvy and fierce ambition stoked a rivalry with Maxfield that ran through the end of the century in Naples, mirroring the competition between Pleasant Valley and Urbana in Hammondsport.

As the culture of wine and grapes matured, it began to generate its own literature—like a good cover crop, plowing experience and skills

FIGURE 3.7. The Widmer family in 1893, Swiss immigrants five years after starting their Naples winery with two casks of Catawba and Concord. On his mother's lap, baby Will would eventually study winemaking at Germany's prestigious Geisenheim Institute and turn Widmer's into the Finger Lake's most innovative winery. His siblings were all pulled out of school at age 16 to work in the vineyard and (the boys only) ultimately in the winery, under Will. *(Courtesy of Hazlitt Red Cat Cellars)*

back into the field. A. L. Underhill, a relative of the Hudson Valley vineyard pioneers, began publishing *The Pleasant Valley Fruit & Wine Reporter* in 1870. A pamphlet of news and technical innovation, it was the first American journal devoted to viticulture and wine. An early edition described the procedure used by Pulteney grower J. Wagener to field-graft part of the seminal vineyard planted by Andrew Reisinger 16 years earlier, changing the variety from Catawba to Iona:

> The entire fruit of a vineyard can be changed to any more desired variety without the loss of a single crop and with little expense, or outlay of labor . . . The interest our several wine companies take in this method is very great . . . It is an advance step in vine culture that will go far toward annihilating the heretofore fabulous prices at which new and choice grape roots have been sold.

Growers around Penn Yan had their own journal on grape culture, *The Vineyardist*, published by attorney and Seneca Lake Wine Co. president J. H. Butler in the 1880s. Groups like the Hammondsport and Lake Keuka Grape Growers Association started running grape fairs at harvest time and sponsoring trade conferences that attracted farmers and scientists from around the country.

In 1882 the state established an Agricultural Experiment Station on the outskirts of Geneva. Research initially focused on dairy but included a vineyard for variety tests and gradually shifted over the years toward pomology and viticulture, responding to the exponential growth of vineyards (and orchards) around the lakes. There were more than 24,000 acres of grapevines by 1890. There were now also more than 50 wineries operating on four lakes; two dozen in the Hammondsport area alone and just two of those—Pleasant Valley and Urbana—together produced more than a million bottles of sparkling wine annually.

Even so, the majority of area vineyards still supplied not the wineries but the fresh fruit market. Of 35,000 tons of grapes grown in the Finger Lakes district in 1890, according to the U. S. Census of Agriculture 80 percent went to the fresh market. Temperance advocates in the state legislature used these data to keep funding for the

Picking Grapes In Snow Storm

FIGURE 3.8. Women were essentially barred from working in 19ᵗʰ century wine cellars but they did much of the work in the vineyards, including harvesting in sometimes-miserable conditions. This and jobs in grape-packing houses enabled a small step toward their emancipation from the home. The light area on the upper left isn't sky but snow-shrouded lake. *(Courtesy of the Steuben County Historical Society)*

Experiment Station directed to crop research and away from wine. A decade earlier, the California legislature had directed the University of California to begin researching and teaching winemaking as well as viticulture. Although winegrowing in California started in earnest around the same time as New York, in the 1850s, by now it was far ahead in acreage, production, and political clout.

New York vineyards at this time still averaged a harvest of only one-and-a-half tons per acre. While viticultural practices had steadily improved, the struggles against vine diseases and insect pests brought on by monoculture left yields little-changed in 50 years. Hand bellows had been used to dust vines with sulfur since the early days in Hammondsport, attempting to control powdery mildew, but sulfur did little to fight rot or discourage insects. By the 1890s hand-pump backpack sprayers and the first horse-powered spray rigs came into the picture, applying a toxic concoction of powdered lead and arsenic, as an insecticide, and a new French discovery, a combination of copper sulfate and lime called Bordeaux mixture. It targeted the two vine diseases—downy mildew and black rot—that had ravaged Nicholas Longworth's Ohio vineyards three decades earlier. Bordeaux mix saved the crop on farms using it during the abominably wet season of 1889, the year it was introduced in New York. It marked a turning point for eastern viticulture, and it may well have saved New York vineyards from the fate of southern Ohio.

Vineyard acreage continued to grow through the end of the century, most of the new plantings now going in on Seneca Lake and seeping east to Cayuga. Some of these were large spreads: 255 acres at the Seneca Lake Grape Vineyard Co. in Romulus; 180 acres at Boyer Diamond Vineyard in Covert; 134 acres at the King Vineyard below Trumansburg. Seneca County between northern Seneca and Cayuga Lakes had 6,000 acres of vineyard in 1894, nearly all of them shipping out fresh fruit from railroad depots. But grape acreage and production in California had surged ahead of the rest of the country. During the 1880s railroads started bringing the new Thompson Seedless California table grape to eastern markets in long-haul refrigerated cars. Faced with this new competition, the packing houses could no longer pay top dollar to growers, releasing better grapes and more grapes to the wineries.

It was not all good news for winemakers. The prominence of the fresh fruit industry had skewed new grape plantings over the years toward Concord, preeminent among table grapes but a second-rate variety for wine. In the 1893 book, *American Grape Growing and Wine Making*, by the leading American viticulturist George Husmann, Concord placed first in his listing of Finger Lakes grape varieties by acreage: Concord, Catawba, Delaware, Isabella, Clinton, Ives, Diana, Elvira, Iona, Eumelan, Niagara, Norton, Moore's Diamond. A decade earlier Concord ranked fifth.

The abundance of Concord grapes brought the Welch Company to New York State in 1896. The ardently anti-alcohol dentists Thomas Welch and his son Charles had launched an "unfermented wine" business in New Jersey in the 1870s, the first commercial application of Louis Pasteur's research on fermentation (and how it could be pre-

FIGURE 3.9. Three dozen men paused for a photograph as they excavated cavernous cellars, expanding the Pleasant Valley Wine Company, in 1889. Blocks of shale dug out of the hill were stacked in "windrows" to be resurrected as winery walls. *(Courtesy of the Steuben County Historical Society)*

vented). Until then there had been no way to stop juice from turning to vinegar or wine; commercial grape juice didn't exist, including what was used at church communions. At first the Welches had trouble convincing their own Methodist Church to replace sacramental wine with their dubious new product.

When the juice business did take hold, it soon outstripped the local supply of grapes. The Welches began buying fruit from Seneca Lake, finally moving the whole business to the head of the lake at Watkins Glen. But between fresh fruit packers and wineries, the unfermented-wine men found the local business climate too competitive. Some wineries like Taylor were also selling grape juice. After a one-year flirtation, the Welch Company packed up and moved west to Chautauqua County.

The popularity of grape juice was being driven by the temperance movement, a powerful force on the American scene by the end of the nineteenth century. The movement's message had long since escalated from a plea for moderation, to a campaign against hard spirits, to a demand for prohibition of alcohol in any form. Kansas had become the first state to constitutionally ban alcohol in 1880. Others were following; New York would not. The 1890 U. S. Census of Agriculture certified New York as the nation's second-ranked wine producer after California. Three-quarters of all the sparkling wine made in the United States came from Keuka Lake.

At the north end of the lake, Penn Yan became the Finger Lakes' third wine village during the boom years of the 1880s. It was already embedded in vines. Young entrepreneurs Frank G. Hallett and A. Clinton Brooks started making wine on a shoestring budget in the cellar of a store on Main Street in 1886, proclaiming their little venture the Empire State Wine Company. They caught the attention of investors looking to repeat what had transpired at the lake's other end.

The newly capitalized company bought and planted vineyards on the bluff between Keuka's two arms and in 1896 began laying up four-foot-thick stone walls for a three-story wine house on Penn Yan's lakefront. The specialty of the house, keying off Keuka Lake's now well-established reputation, was sparkling wine. A 1906 catalogue of the Keuka region's champagne-makers ranked the ten–year-old Empire State winery number five, at 5,000 cases—a notch below Hammondsport's Germania Cellars. The company had recently purchased the vineyards and what was left of Seneca Lake's winery on Severne Point after a spectacular fire.

Despite its thick walls, the Penn Yan winery's construction above ground on a level site caused problems from the start, especially on hot summer days when temperatures in the riddling storage rooms crept up. *The Penn Yan Democrat* routinely reported injuries from exploding bottles; fermenting and aging in glass, sparkling wine was terminally vulnerable to changes in pressure brought about by rising temperature.

There was trouble outside the winery as well. On a too-frequent occasion around the turn of the century, the *Democrat* wrote "a serious perhaps fatal runaway occurred about noon today. A wagon belonging to the Empire State Wine company was being loaded at the wine cellar when the team ran away down Lake Street frightened by the explosion of a bottle of wine . . . Near the schoolhouse the team ran into a wagon loaded with peaches driven by Mrs. Benjamin Dean and the impact threw Mrs. Dean to the ground." Not long after this the company purchased "a state-of-the-art, 20-ton ammonia refrigeration machine that can keep all its wine vaults and cellars at an even temperature during the hot months." The earth-cooled cellar of ancient times was giving way to twentieth-century technology.

Fire was another hazard plaguing the wineries, periodically reducing operations to hollow stone shells. The straw used to pack champagne bottles made perfect tinder for igniting cellars full of wooden equipment. When Pulteney Wine Cellars went up in flames, 40,000

FIGURE 3.10. A German baker named Jacob Frey started making wine in a vault under his Hammondsport Hotel in 1879. The following year he bought land next to the Pleasant Valley Wine Company and started building cellars, adding to them nearly every year as the business flourished until it looked like this a decade later. Germania's verandas were packed with spectators in 1908 when Glenn Curtiss piloted the "June Bug" over the valley flats, the first public flight of an airplane. (*Courtesy of the Steuben County Historical Society*)

gallons of wine ran into the winery's drywell. Firefighters arrived too late for the winery but they pumped wine from the well to save a neighbor's house.

The Seneca Lake Wine Company suffered through two disastrous fires; one of them destroyed 100,000 gallons of wine, including 40,000 bottles of champagne. Fire weakened the company, sent it through a succession of salvage owners, and eventually burned it to a ruin.

On a June morning in 1906 Hammondsporters living near the lake woke up to find its headwaters turned blood red. A fire at the Monarch winery had sent 50,000 gallons of wine spilling into Cold Brook and on down Keuka Inlet through the village to the lake.

A young horticulturist named Ulysses Prentiss Hedrick came to the Geneva Agricultural Experiment Station in 1905 to oversee its fruit breeding program, which included a small experiment with European vinifera vines. Fourteen varieties grafted on native American rootstock had been planted at the station in 1902; only one survived the first winter. Another five varieties were put in the following year, this time laid down on the ground for the winter and covered with an insulating blanket of soil. They succeeded and Hedrick inherited a fragile but healthy little vinifera vineyard that would now face the challenge of reaching full maturity, something European vines had failed to achieve in eastern America.

Burying vines for winter protection was a practice already well-known to growers on cold sites, even with native varieties. Grafting European-variety vines on native-grape rootstock resistant to insect pests had also been done for many years. A breakthrough at the Geneva station came with use of the still relatively new fungicide Bordeaux mix to protect critically vulnerable European vines from mildew and rot endemic to America. It was the last missing piece in the agonizing, intractable puzzle to grow the grapes of the Old World in the New.

When Hedrick declared his vines fully mature and "growing vigorously" in 1911, the station forged ahead with a test of no less than 100 vinifera varieties. For the first time in 300 years of effort, European grapevines had taken up long-term residence in an eastern American vineyard. "Old fallacies have received many hard knocks,"

Hedrick wrote, "and chains of tradition in which the culture of plants was bound, have been broken . . . European grapes may now be grown successfully in eastern America."

It could be done; but there were clearly still more challenges and risks than with native varieties, and the apparent need to bury vines for winter protection would continue to discourage commercial growers in the Finger Lakes and other northern areas for years to come.

During this work with vinifera, a time when he was also busy hybridizing new varieties, Hedrick published his landmark study, *The Grapes of New York*, an astonishing accomplishment coming less than three years after he had moved to the state from Michigan (he did have four collaborators). It was the first book of a series he would produce on various fruits. Its 564 pages surveyed the geology and climate of the state's vineyard districts, reviewed its viticultural history, and catalogued more than 1,400 grape varieties encompassing accidental crosses of European and native grapes and the voluminous output of hybridizers over the preceding century. Hedrick's was the first great work of viticultural scholarship to come out of New York since William Prince's 1830 *Treatise on the Vine*.

The arrival of Paul Garrett in the Finger Lakes in 1912 was akin to the arrival of the first automobile in a town that had known only the horse and carriage. By now the area's top wineries were selling in many states around the country, but Garrett was mid-stream in the creation of America's first nationwide wine empire.

He was a southern gentleman from North Carolina, where he started working in his family's winery in 1877 at the age of 14. By 1903 he was running five operations around that state making wine from the inimitable Scuppernong grape, a variety of vitis peculiar to the South. He labeled the wine "Virginia Dare," named after the first child born to English settlers in the New World, on Carolina's Roanoke Island. Ablaze with Scuppernong's perfume and fruitiness, Virginia Dare was unlike any other wine on the market and it became a huge hit nationwide. When demand outpaced the capabilities of southern vineyards, Garrett began blending with New York and California wine, for which he pioneered the cross-country transport of wine in railroad tank cars. Winemaking was becoming more uncoupled from the vineyard.

But Paul Garrett became a fugitive of Prohibition. When North Carolina banned wine in 1908 he moved his fermentations across the state line to Norfolk, Virginia. He was buying New York juice and wine from the Empire State Wine Company in Penn Yan. In 1912 he hired the founder and manager of that company, Frank Hallett, to ensconce Garrett & Company in the Finger Lakes. Within a few years Hallett had facilities operating in Penn Yan, Canandaigua, Hammondsport, and Naples.

The Finger Lakes had not seen anything like it. Garrett's plants were filled with glass-lined concrete tanks. The central production building in Penn Yan housed a mammoth wine press capable of

FIGURE 3.11. Looking north at the bluff between Keuka Lake's two arms, the hillsides were quilted with vineyards in the years before Prohibition. This photograph may well have been taken from one of Glenn Curtiss's early airplanes. Steamboats like the one off Bluff Point were at the end of their run as workhorses of the lake's commerce and tourism. (*Courtesy of the Fred and Harriet Taylor Memorial Library*)

processing seven-and-a-half tons an hour. A fleet of 30 glass-lined, 10,000-gallon tank cars took wine by rail to Norfolk for blending and bottling, until Virginia in its turn went dry. Garrett then made Penn Yan the headquarters of a national enterprise that included 17 wine and grape-juice plants in North Carolina, Virginia, New York, Ohio, Missouri, and California—total capacity 10 million gallons.

Virginia Dare was now America's best-selling wine. Scuppernong had dwindled to a minor ingredient; most of the wine's high-powered fruitiness now came from the Concord and Catawba school of Finger Lakes *labrusca* grapes. Garrett looked over his far-flung wine empire from an elegant home on the lip of Keuka Lake's Bluff Point.

From there he could also look down across the vine-draped water toward a nation steadily going dry, obsessed with a crusade against alcohol and resolved to destroy the life and work he had known since childhood. As the nation's leading winemaker, he would take on the role of chief industry spokesman and impassioned, hapless defender against the juggernaut of national Prohibition.

CHAPTER 4

Western New York

In the Genesee Valley, the Finger Lakes, the Hudson Valley, the roots of winegrowing in New York were nourished by the church. It was true again, with a special irony, at the state's western end on Lake Erie.

For many years historians believed the state's first winery opened in the Hudson Valley village of Washingtonville, in 1839. But a few years before the first vintage at John Jaques winery, a homesteader in another valley, west of the Finger Lakes, placed an advertisement in a religious periodical for "York Wine."

The Genesee Valley was the first area of the state's western Indian Territory to open for settlement after the Revolutionary War. Samuel Warren arrived there as an 18-year-old farmhand in 1816, saved enough in one year to buy land in what would become the township of York, and planted his first grapevines in the late 1820s, about the same time William Bostwick was adding grapes to his garden in Hammondsport. The intention of both men was to make wine for church sacraments, but Warren, a deacon of the Congregational Church, meant to make it his business. When he built a house for his young family in 1834 he dug the cellar deep enough to accommodate three tiers of wine barrels. In two years it held the five barrels of York wine offered for sale in the *New York Evangelist.*

In 20 years Warren's sons Josiah and Harlan were running the business and the cellar was filled with 3,400 gallons made from their own expanding vineyard and grapes bought from friends inspired by the Warrens' example. One of them, Moses Long, started his own winery nearby. At about the same time, the Genesee River town of Avon became the center of vineyards and wine cellars supplying the clientele of resort spas dominating that village. Records of Avon wine were lost in village fires but the vineyards were well-known when Andrew Reisinger came for cuttings in 1855, to plant the first vines on slopes south of Hammondsport.

Josiah Warren moved his family business from the York farmhouse cellar into a new stone winery during the Civil War. By that time York Wines offered a dozen different varietals to the pharmacy trade as well as to churches. Josiah's brother Harlan took over when he came back from the war, adding a cider mill, but the business became entangled in a railroad right-of-way dispute that eventually cleaved the property with train tracks. The coming of the railroad breathed new life into many struggling enterprises but for the Warrens it drained life away. A Livingston County historian wrote the post-mortem: "[H]aving secured the right-of-way and run their tracks directly through this once interesting spot, the buildings are no longer in use and all the prolific vines have been exterminated." In the end Harlan Warren was found dead, hanging from a rafter in his abandoned winery.

Josiah had meanwhile relocated to the Rochester area, drawn there by a wine operation on Lake Ontario's Irondequoit Bay. This was the business of Joseph Vinton, who had settled on the bay in 1812 when its hilly shores were still wilderness. He built a sawmill and the forest fell to the blade, supplying lumber to build the new Genesee River–Erie Canal city of Rochesterville. In 1841 when the hills along the bay were all cleared, the resourceful Vinton converted his sawmill into a hotel, the Newport House. He terraced the surrounding slope and began lining it with grapevines.

Rochester had by then become a center of horticultural enterprise. The *Genesee Farmer and Gardener's Journal* started publishing there in 1831, providing a clearinghouse of information encouraging farmers and homesteaders to, among other endeavors, plant grapes and make wine. Hammondsport's William Bostwick was a frequent contributor. The Monroe Garden and Nurseries was the first of many nurseries to open in the area. It issued a catalogue for the 1841–42 season listing dozens of native grape varieties each tagged with a recommendation either for fresh fruit or for wine.

Vinton planted Isabellas and a new variety developed in nearby Lyons—Oporto—so-named to promise a good dark port wine. Hedrick's *Grapes of New York* later dismissed it as an inferior, excessively vigorous variety but Joseph Vinton gave Oporto a good run on Irondequoit Bay; his blend with Isabella became a big success labeled Irondequoit Port.

Josiah Warren bought Vinton's 45-acre vineyard and wine business in 1865 with a partner, Asa McBride, a young wine salesman from Hammondsport. Together they added vineyards ramping up from the waters of the bay and encircling a new fieldstone wine cellar. McBride went on to grow the business to well over 100,000 gallons annual production, adding another 50 acres of vines and a second wine cellar on Canandaigua Lake. For its two facilities the Irondequoit Wine Company purchased 600 tons of grapes each fall from Genesee Valley and Finger Lakes growers, and dispatched half a dozen salesmen across the United States.

FIGURE 4.1. An ink-blotter advertisement shows the Irondequoit Wine Company's cellar and vineyards ramping down to Lake Ontario's Irondequoit Bay. The date of establishment, 1832, probably refers to another winery run by one of Irondequoit's owners, Josiah Warren. (*Courtesy of the Town of York Historical Society*)

The Irondequoit vineyard at Newport House spun off a community of Rochester area wine ventures. The Dubelbeiss Winery was perhaps the most admired. A German-Swiss immigrant named Samuel Dubelbeiss, from a family of winemakers dating back to the fourteenth century, settled near Vinton's sawmill in 1839. He became the area's first wine merchant, observed the development of Vinton's wine estate, and helped his son Louis plant a vineyard adjacent to the Irondequoit Wine Company in the early 1870s. Their cobblestone winery on Ridge Road East sold dry, "Du Belle" wines exclusively to private homes; unusual in its day.

One of Joseph Vinton's employees, George Beck, went off on his own in the 1850s to plant a vineyard on Ontario's shore at Charlotte. He was advertising his wines in Rochester and Buffalo newspapers by 1861. When he died in the 1880s, an inventory of thousands of gallons of Beck wines seeded another operation, the Ontario Wine Company in Greece. The Genesee Valley Wine Company also got started at about this time, based in Rochester but linked through one of its owners, Isaac Seeley, to his vineyards and winery in Vine Valley on Canandaigua Lake. Connections between Rochester investors and Finger Lakes vineyards became common in the late 1800s; the Genesee Valley company also merged for a while with the Seneca Lake winery at Severne Point. That alliance terminated with a fire, and the Canandaigua merger ended badly, too, when legal wrangling led one Rochester investor to launch a moonlight raid on the inventory in Seeley's Vine Valley cellar. Wine could draw people together and the money wine made could throw them apart.

Fifty miles south of Rochester another horticultural and viticultural hotspot developed in the mid- to late-1800s at the village of Dansville. This was the tip of Lake Ontario's benign influence on the Genesee Valley climate. Nurseries were Dansville's heartbeat; they laid a quilt of fruit trees, berry patches, and vines across the broad, flat corridor north of town. On the long hill flanking the east side of town, in 1860, Dr. F. M. Perine set out an 8-acre vineyard behind the Jackson Sanitorium, testing the prospects for Catawba, Isabella, Diana, Concord and Delaware. His medical practice at the sanitorium promoted the Grape Cure, the fashionable fresh-fruit diet on the last leg of its migration from Europe to New York City and on into the countryside.

Perine had more in mind than fresh fruit; when all his varieties did well he started making wine. This attracted the notice of three Germans from Keuka Lake: John "Fritz" Michael, Andrew Freidell, and Jacob Smith. Freidell's brother Mathias had just opened a winery in the village of Hammondsport. Together the three established a 15-acre vineyard adjacent to Perine's, with the same varieties. As always, more followed. The hillside was gradually striped top-to-bottom with vines, including several more blocks planted by Perine and one operated by the Jackson Sanitorium itself. There were 200 acres on East Hill by the turn of the century, and half a dozen small wineries. Perine's, one of the biggest, made 3,000 to 4,000 gallons a year.

As in Rochester, the Dansville winegrowers would flourish for a few decades, struggle into the twentieth century, but never achieve the critical mass needed to weather national Prohibition. They became the curiosities of old photographs.

Another, smaller community of grape growers clustered around the Erie Canal town of Lockport, between Rochester and Buffalo. A few of them formed a cooperative winery in the 1860s on a hill north of the village. It didn't last, but Lockport still made viticultural history with the introduction of the Niagara grape variety by horticulturist Wheaton Clarke and nurseryman Claudius Hoag in 1882. Clarke crossed Concord with the little-known Cassady variety and came up with a white analogue of the phenomenally successful Concord. By teaming up with a nurseryman and incorporating their operation as the Niagara Grape Company, Clarke was able to maintain tight control of planting material. Aggressively promoted but not available through every nursery catalogue in circulation, Niagara took on the marketing cachet of exclusivity. It quickly dominated plantings along Lake Ontario and spread to the Finger Lakes, where Jacob Widmer put it in his new vineyard at Naples. The Niagara Grape Company owned a controlling interest in many local vineyards.

Nearly every new variety experienced a trough of reality behind the wave of introduction. When mature vines started revealing Niagara's weaknesses—it was less cold hardy and disease resistant than Concord—

FIGURE 4.2. German immigrant John "Fritz" Michael tended vineyards on the hillside above the Livingston County town of Dansville in the late 1800s. Michael's was one of more than half a dozen small wineries in Dansville. The town's celebrated Jackson Sanatorium, partly visible in the distance, had its own vineyards. (*Courtesy of Jane Schryver*)

growers had second thoughts. Along the Ontario shore many of them were primarily orchardists only speculating in grapes, easily spooked by the Niagara bubble. Fruit trees remained the district's focus.

To their credit, Clarke and Hoag were trying to guard against the fate of too many grape hybridizers who toiled for years or decades to bring forward a promising new variety, only to see it swallowed into the marketplace of nurseries and the free-for-all of farmers disseminated cuttings, returning little or nothing to the creator. It happened to Ephraim Bull, the man behind Concord, and to A. J. Caywood in the Hudson Valley. It happened also to Jacob Moore, a lifelong nurseryman and hybridizer working in the Rochester satellite town of Brighton. Among many hundreds of trials, Moore crossed Concord with Iona, producing a variety he named Diamond. It was released at the same time as Niagara and was overshadowed, but Diamond ultimately gained recognition as one of the best, most refined native grapes for wine, still and sparkling. Jacob Moore, however, died in poverty.

With Deacon Warren in the Genesee Valley, Reverend Bostwick in the Finger Lakes, John Jaques in the Hudson Valley, the roots of winegrowing in New York were nourished by the church. It was true again, with a special irony, at the state's western end on Lake Erie.

Twenty-year-old Elijah Fay took his bride there from Massachusetts in 1811, building one of the first log cabins at a crossroads that would become the village of Brocton. Fay had a keen interest in grapes. He sent back east for cuttings of the "fox grapes" he knew in Massachusetts, wild labrusca vines; but they failed to mature a crop. He tried again with European varieties; they also failed. In 1824 he bought a few Isabella and Catawba vines from the Prince nursery on Long Island and the Lake Erie Grape Belt was born.

Fay was a founder and deacon of Brocton's First Baptist Church, where parishioners taking communion sipped Catawba wine from Fay's 10-gallon vintage of 1830. This was still a few years before Warren's first wine in York, Bostwick's in Hammondsport, and Jaques's in Washingtonville. Over the years Fay added more backyard vines, sending at least one batch of fruit by boat to a dubious market in Buffalo. "What are they good for? How do you use them?" were some of the comments at his street stall. From the rest of his crop each year he made a hundred gallons of wine.

Fay's son Joseph and nephew Lincoln were the first enthusiasts to pick up vine culture around Brocton. Lincoln would introduce to the area a new variety called Concord in the late 1850s. Joseph planted the region's first commercial-scale vineyard in 1851, initially selling fresh fruit but, in an 1859 partnership with his brother-in-law Garrett Ryckman and a friend, Rufus Haywood, Joseph gambled his crop into the region's first commercial vintage—2,000 gallons of Catawba and Isabella. The three men had ambitious plans for Brocton Wine Cellars, beginning with the excavation of a double-level cellar, each one ten feet high for European-style oval tanks. Pooling the resources and talents of colleagues carried the business forward just as it did, about the same time, at the Finger Lakes' Pleasant Valley Wine Company.

Thomas Quigley opened his Wine House in Brocton a few years after Fay and partners started the Brocton cellars. Grape growers Jonas Martin and Ralph Fuller soon followed; there would eventually

FIGURE 4.3. Garrett Ryckman bought out two partners in Chautauqua County's first wine venture before building this "modern" winery, photographed here in the mid-1870s. The original wood-frame Brocton Wine Cellar is just visible as a wing in the back. Ryckman and his son dominated the Chautauqua wine scene for 50 years. (*Private collection, Used with Permission*)

be close to a dozen wineries clustered around Brocton and its sister-village Portland.

Virtually all the early Lake Erie wineries ran in tandem with the marketing of fresh grapes, growers typically making wine from culled grapes and surplus fruit. The mainstay varieties, Catawba and Isabella, fell into a mix with Delaware, Concord, Iona, Worden, and others. Winemaking operations began opening up in Fredonia and Westfield.

Thomas Lake Harris arrived in Chautauqua County from the Hudson Valley with his entourage, the Brotherhood of the New Life, in 1867. After Amenia this was the Brotherhood's fourth home in less than ten years, chosen for Chautauqua's unique mix of evangelical ferment and burgeoning vineyards—fertile ground for Harris's iconoclastic wine business. One of his followers, English aristocrat Lady Maria Oliphant, sold her jewelry to buy 2,100-acres of farmland between Brocton and a two-mile stretch of lake shore. Harris named it "The Use." Two hundred members proceeded to plant vineyards and build stone-arched cellars, with assurances to local temperance folk that this would be wine "filled with the divine breath so that all noxious influences are neutralized."

Harris hired a German winemaker from Missouri, where the wine industry had grown to become, briefly, the biggest in America on the strength of that state's German immigrants. Production at The Use's Lake Erie and Missouri Wine Company rose to 20,000 gallons, far more than Harris had made in Amenia but still never enough to support the commune.

Harris was a particularly controversial figure within the spiritualist, occult, and other evangelical eruptions of the day, not least for his winemaking but also for his cigar-smoking authoritarian style and quirky sexual proclamations (he declared himself "a divine man-woman" and tried at times to enforce Shaker-style celibate marriage). His mesmerizing, extemporaneous, hours-long sermons—by all accounts they were ethereal adventures—carried The Use along for more than a decade, but mounting debts and dissension in the ranks finally caused the colony to fall apart in 1883. By then Harris had already abandoned ship for California.

Winds of change blew through the new Chautauqua–Erie Grape Belt in the 1870s, including frigid blasts in December of 1872 announcing the coldest winter in anyone's memory. Grapevines were hit hard, crops wiped out, entire vineyards killed to the ground. Only one variety pulled through in good enough shape to put money in growers' pockets the next fall: New England-bred Concord.

During the sad summer of 1873, as growers contemplated rows of dead vines, *The Fredonia Censor* reported that "a committee of six ladies went around to see the liquor dealers." They politely requested that the village's saloon-keepers, hotels and pharmacists take a pledge to cease selling alcohol except, in the case of pharmacies, with a doctor's prescription. As the numbers and tactics of their petitioners escalated, many pharmacies complied. However "the hotels and saloons refuse to quit," as the *Censor* put it, "but the ball is still rolling." By year's end a headline declared "The Women are Marching—Over a Hundred Strong!" Some of the women were wives of grape farmers; they began lobbying their husbands to reject wine varieties and plant the table grape Concord. Had the winter laid out God's own viticultural design for Chautauqua? There were 500 acres of Concord vines in the Grape Belt in 1870; by decade's end there were 14,000.

The most powerful engine behind this Concord juggernaut came on steel rails. The lake plain along Erie's shore was the chosen route for three railroad trunk lines connecting northeastern cities through Buffalo to Cleveland, Chicago, and the west; rail-lines that perfectly skewered the length of the Chautauqua–Erie grape district. With the introduction of stackable "Climax" wooden grape baskets in the 1870s, what had been bushel boatloads to Buffalo could now access a national marketplace. Jonas Martin sent the first full railcar of grapes to Philadelphia in 1877. He partnered with Garrett Ryckman to ship eight carloads the next year, and before long the railroads were building sidings with loading docks in the midst of vineyards along the length of the grape belt. By the late 1880s thousands of carloads of grapes, stacked under roof bunkers filled with Lake Erie ice, went to market every fall all over the eastern half of the nation.

Railroad construction crews brought into the area a community of Italian immigrants, who of course brought with them a requirement for wine. The sight of a sea of vines must have been comforting, but the Chautauqua wineries were mainly making sweet and fortified wines, and brandy. At Garrett Ryckman & Son's Brocton Cellars, in the 1880s, nearly all their output consisted of Port, Sherry and Sweet Catawba. The Lake Erie Wine Company's list of Westfield wines was typical: White Tokay, Golden Sherry, Port, Sweet Catawba, Sweet Iona.

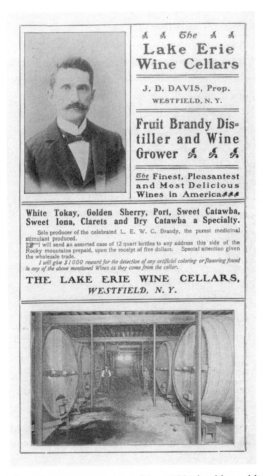

FIGURE 4.4. This advertisement appeared in a 1901 booklet published by the Chautauqua Grape & Wine Association to promote the county's fruit-based industry at the Pan-American Exposition in Buffalo. Running ads for juice makers, fresh grapes, and wine, the association straddled a widening rift between winemakers and prohibitionists.

This was not what Italians drank with dinner. Many of them chose to settle around Fredonia and make it their own wine town. Peter Lanza, LaGrasso & Co., the Rosso Brothers, Peter Elardo, G. Blande—by century's end their cellars produced each year something over 200,000 gallons of dry wine—the locals called it sour wine.

In the 1880s and 90s most of the wineries, minus the Italians, added grape juice to their lists of wines and table grapes. New enterprises were opening with unfermented juice as their only product. The Gleason Fruit Juice Co. in Ripley called it "Grapine"—a drink to nourish the shifting sentiment in Chautauqua society from moderation and temperance toward prohibition.

Into this heady mix of juice, brandy, table grapes by the carload, sweet and sour wine came The Welch Company in 1897, relocating from a false start in the Finger Lakes. Here the staunchly anti-alcohol dentists-turned-juice-makers found their true home. A 1901 pamphlet described the company's new Westfield headquarters, "a three-story brick factory with immense cellars and an annual output of 125,000 gallons. They have invaded the English market and are getting a strong hold across the water. They run a printing establishment which turns out their advertising matter and is of itself a big industry." Their advertisements trumpeted "an unequaled temperance drink for the home."

Through the turn of the century Garrett Ryckman and his sons continued to dominate regional winemaking with their original Brocton Cellars and a second operation at the Lake Shore Wine Company. The two facilities accounted for a quarter of the district's total wine production of nearly two million gallons in 1904, about as high as it would go. Five years later a spectacular fire destroyed the 50-year-old Brocton winery and its entire inventory, incinerating the heart of the Chautauqua–Erie wine industry. Although the Ryckmans rebuilt the winery it never regained its footing, eventually becoming a satellite plant for The Welch Company, a marker in the transition sweeping the region. The combined forces of grape juice, table grapes and temperance were slowly squeezing wine out of the Lake Erie Grape Belt.

CHAPTER 5

Collision of Cultures

After one year from the ratification of this article, the manufacture, sale, or transportation of intoxicating liquors within, the importation thereof into, or the exportation thereof from the United States and all territory subject to its jurisdiction thereof for beverage purposes is hereby prohibited.

—18th Amendment to the U. S. Constitution

The genesis of the Temperance movement in America had little to do with wine; it was a response to the alarming indulgence in hard liquor and its consequences for the young country's social fabric and economic function. The colonial taste for hard cider and rum was giving way to whiskey by the late eighteenth century. Wine was relatively scarce, mostly limited to Madeira on the sideboards of the well-to-do and French clarets in the cellars of epicures like Thomas Jefferson and Benjamin Franklin.

In 1791 Tench Coxe, an Assistant Secretary of the Treasury under Alexander Hamilton and one of the leading economists of the day, drew up an itemized plan for a model agricultural settlement hypothetically located along the Susquehanna River in either Pennsylvania or New York State. It called for 800 houses, one grist mill, one brewery, *ten* distilleries, no winery. This must surely have set Thomas Jefferson's teeth on edge; Jefferson who famously wrote "no nation is drunken where wine is cheap, and none sober where the dearness of wine substitutes ardent spirits as the common beverage. It [wine] is, in truth, the only antidote to the bane of whiskey."

As Coxe wrote his report, Jefferson's good friend Dr. Benjamin Rush, the new nation's medical conscience, published *An Inquiry into the Effects of Spiritous Liquors*. It too bemoaned "the depradations of ardent spirits" and made the case for wine as the drink of moderation. Rush and Jefferson, unfortunately, were voices in a wilderness of distilleries; by 1810 there were more than 14,000 scattered through the country, and one winery. Between 1800 and 1830, rough estimates suggest Americans over the age of 14 averaged a staggering annual per capita consumption of about seven gallons of pure alcohol, a rate much higher than at any other time in American history. Drunkenness, alcoholism, broken families, domestic abuse were rampant. And alcohol-soaked political campaigns suggested government was not likely to do much about it. George Washington himself set out bowls of rum at Mt. Vernon campaign rallies when he ran for Virginia's House of Burgesses.

The men who worked on America's new canals were notorious binge drinkers. When the Erie Canal connected to Keuka Lake and the young Finger Lakes village of Hammondsport, taverns sprouted along Water Street to serve "canalers." There were routine drunken brawls. Someone would eventually knock over an oil lamp setting the tavern on fire and, too often, the entire street went up in flames. Every few years downtown Hammondsport had to be rebuilt, until village elders finally threw up their hands and relocated the entire business district, minus the taverns, to a new town square away from canal docks on the lake.

The earliest recorded, organized response to this kind of mayhem came in 1808 when a physician near Glens Falls, B. J. Clark, "saw that unless something could be done to arrest the progress of dram-drinking," according to *The Methodist Magazine and Quarterly Review*, "all the skill he could exert in his profession could not save the people from a premature grave and interminable ruin." First in line among those at risk were the hard-drinking lumbermen working in the surrounding Adirondack foothills. Dr. Clark helped form the Moreau Temperance Association, a loose-knit group meeting regularly to pledge their abstinence from liquor. It operated as a kind of support-group precursor of Alcoholics Anonymous, but wine and beer were not targeted.

A few years later a group of Boston patricians formed The Massachusetts Society for the Suppression of Intemperance. Their motivation was more managerial than moral: to boost the productivity of the labor force. Again the focus was on hard spirits; the society's principals sipped wine at their meetings.

Local initiatives like these coalesced into the American Temperance Union in 1833, where disagreement soon surfaced over just how much and what kinds of alcohol could be tolerated—questions that would percolate in the American psyche for the next hundred years. Lists of Union members began to mark a "T" beside the names of those who favored total abstinence, hence the term "teetotaler" (according to one of several claims for the word's origin). Initially even many of the teetotalers abjured only distilled liquor, but as the movement expanded, advocates of moderation and tolerance for wine and beer steadily lost influence to hardliners.

When Livingston County winemaker Samuel Warren placed his ad in an 1836 issue of *The Evangelist* newspaper for sacramental wine, it provoked a storm of controversy. It did not appear again. A few years later in Hammondsport a militant teetotaler ripped the grapevines out of Reverend Bostwick's rectory garden. The vestments of the church offered no protection from those who saw the devil's business in any form of alcohol.

Temperance meetings, revivals, fiery sermons, church pamphlets— the grassroots campaign against alcohol informed a striking change in the country's drinking habits. By 1845 per capita alcohol consumption had dropped by two-thirds.

The Temperance movement was embedded in the evangelical and social reform movements of the day: anti-slavery, women's rights, health and education reform, utopian communities, the birth of two (anti-alcohol) religious sects in western New York—the Mormons and Seventh-Day Adventists. High-profile reformers, including Susan B. Anthony, Frederick Douglass, and Elizabeth Cady Stanton, spoke passionately about the evils of alcohol, in Stanton's case from grim experience: her second husband had been murdered in a drunken rage by the man she had divorced.

In 1845 the New York legislature passed a law restricting "the public sale" of liquor. It was repealed two years later, but the issue was far from dead. Stanton and Anthony organized the Women's State Temperance Society of New York to lobby in Albany, where Stanton appealed to a session of the legislature in 1853 to enact prohibition statutes modeled after those recently adopted in Maine, the first state to ban intoxicating liquor. The following year New York again passed restrictions on liquor distribution. They were overturned by the courts.

The admission of new states into the union set a fire under the issue of slavery, ignited in Kansas and Missouri. As reformers began to focus their efforts on abolition, the crusade against alcohol lost steam. The Civil War years obscured virtually every social issue except slavery; women were busy running households while men went off to war. To help finance the war President Lincoln called for an excise tax on the production of spirits, beer, and wine, the first such levy since the Whiskey Tax of 1791. Advocates of prohibition ironically opposed the tax more vociferously than beverage makers did, arguing that it would give government a vested interest in alcohol.

After the war the saloon became a fixture of the nation's towns and cities and alcohol consumption again began to climb. Historians link much of this to the social impacts of industrialization and immigration; the saloon became the refuge of the working man and the immigrant underclass—the poor man's social club. It presented an urgent, easy target for the resurgence of prohibitionist sentiment. The movement found its flashpoint in the religious fervor of western New York's "burned over district"—so-called for the fiery sermons raging through its towns. The Women's Crusade of 1873–74 began in that part of the state the day six ladies marched out of their Methodist church to confront Fredonia's tavern owners and pharmacies. They were the vanguard in a season of women marching on saloons, holding vigils, and staging sit-ins from upstate New York through Ohio and the Midwest, adopting a strategy of occupation that would become a central tool of American protest movements.

In the summer of 1873 a group of women from Fredonia, Jamestown, and other local villages convened at a Sunday School retreat on Chautauqua Lake, where they laid the groundwork for the Woman's Christian Temperance Union (WCTU). Their meeting place became the venerable Chautauqua Institution, a center of the arts and culture with its own enduring ban on alcohol. The WCTU, soon under the leadership of the dynamic Frances Willard, became the nation's most powerful voice against alcohol for many years. Willard broadened its agenda to include progressive issues: women's suffrage (women would overwhelmingly vote Dry) and a national income tax (it would obviate the need for the liquor tax that accounted for a third of federal revenue).

In the early 1880s, even as New York's wineries (and breweries) proliferated into a full-fledged agricultural industry, the WCTU successfully lobbied to prevent any funding for wine research at the state's new Agricultural Experiment Station in Geneva. The Union also petitioned the state legislature to enact a Scientific Temperance Education Bill, passed in 1884, requiring schools to describe alcohol as a poison. Textbooks were officially screened by a WCTU committee.

The election of teetotaler Rutherford Hayes as president drained the nation's first household Dry in 1877. Visiting dignitaries were confounded: "Oh it was very gay," one European ambassador said of a state dinner with the president, "the water flowed like champagne." Four years later New Yorker Chester A. Arthur brought champagne back to the White House and the dispute lurched on.

Waves of European immigration to the United States from the late 1800s through the turn of the century reshaped American drinking habits. Wine played a small part. German winegrowers coming to the Finger Lakes and Italians to Chautauqua County and the Hudson Valley nourished a subculture of wine, but the more significant shift of popular taste went from spirits to beer. In the early 1900s beer accounted for four-fifths of the typical saloon's sales. The consumption of alcohol began to rise again and many in the Prohibition movement blamed immigrants. As America slid toward war with Germany, the country's overwhelmingly German-immigrant-run breweries fused anti-alcohol with anti-immigrant in the minds of many Americans. Prohibitionism took on a nativist rancor.

While these were potent national forces, they had little impact on New York winemakers. Vineyard acreage kept growing and both wine and juice production increased. In 1916 flourishing Finger Lakes wineries doubled the prices paid to grape growers. By that time 27 states had either adopted prohibition or were poised to, but most winemakers dismissed the idea that it could ever happen in New York.

There were more signs of trouble. The insurance industry, an emerging economic force, aligned with prohibitionists in the hope a ban on alcohol would reduce accident and health claims. The American Medical Association followed into the fray in 1917 when it reversed a long, hallowed tradition and flatly declared wine had no medical value.

Understanding, accepting, and preparing for what was coming proved key to a winery's endurance through the grueling years ahead. The immigrant families running many of New York's small operations believed, if Prohibition did come to the entire nation, surely it would not include the beverage of moderation and mealtimes and Old World culture. They felt protected by centuries of tradition. In December of 1917 a group of ten Keuka wineries ran three full-page advertisements in *The Hammondsport Herald* extolling the history and virtues of wine.

The pragmatic businessmen behind Hammondsport's Columbia Wine Co., on the other hand, chose to bail out early. They pressed no grapes from the 1917 harvest, began liquidating their inventory, and put the winery—the first in the state to electrify—up for sale.

Between the extremes of denial and despair, a relatively few winemakers were taking a hard look at what appeared to be their lot and how they might reshape their operations to adapt. They were shifting from a mindset of winemaker-first to businessman-first. John Jacob Widmer was a good example. He had started selling grape juice in addition to wine in 1912. A year before Prohibition took effect Widmer's Wine Cellars constructed a large, separate juice plant next to the winery, equipped it with a pasteurizer, a dealcoholizer, and customized juice-packaging lines. The winery laboratory began to identify and test new products they could make from grapes.

Also in 1919 the Taylor Wine Co. bought the Columbia winery. Taylor's huge winepress along with other equipment and cooperage came down from Bully Hill to the facility south of Hammondsport, and production started shifting from wine to juice, using Columbia's state-of-the-art electric bottling line to begin marketing grape juice, for the first time at Taylor, in glass.

At Keuka Lake's other end, in August of 1919, Paul Garrett was adding an addition to his Penn Yan winery and advertising to buy all the grapes he could "of practically every variety as soon as this year's crop is ripe," on the eve of Prohibition. He planned to make wine at Penn Yan and his other plants, send it by rail to Brooklyn's Bush Terminal and strip out the alcohol to make vanilla flavoring extract and industrial solvents. The dealcoholized wine would become a Prohibition-era incarnation of Virginia Dare.

Congress passed the 18th Amendment to the Constitution in January 1918 and sent it to the states for ratification. Section I read "After one year from the ratification of this article, the manufacture, sale, or transportation of intoxicating liquors within, the importation thereof into, or the exportation thereof from the United States and all territory subject to its jurisdiction thereof for beverage purposes is hereby prohibited." Everyone including the prohibitionist lobby was surprised by how quickly—in one year—the Amendment reached the 36th state approval needed to become the law of the land. New York was not among the 36.

Individual state prohibition laws had explicitly banned wine and beer as well as distilled spirits, but the federal amendment did not define just what it meant by "intoxicating liquors." Winemakers, brewers, and their millions of customers still held out hope for a liberal interpretation until, three months before the ban took effect, Congress passed the National Prohibition Act, called the Volstead Act after its chief sponsor. It defined "intoxicating liquor" as any beverage containing more than one half of one percent alcohol.

The Volstead Act triggered a rush on pharmacies, groceries, and other local wine outlets. When their supplies ran out, people turned to the source, with mounting frenzy as the January 1920 deadline drew nearer. People streamed out of Buffalo, Pittsburgh, and Cleveland to the wineries of Chautauqua–Erie; out of Rochester and Syracuse to Finger Lakes wineries, and from New York City too, once New Yorkers had sucked all the inventory from Hudson Valley cellars. They arrived at winery doors at all hours of the day and night in cars, carriages, trucks, horse-drawn wagons, rented buses, and vans. One man pulled up to the Pleasant Valley Wine Co. in a hearse, stacked it to the roof with cases of sparkling wine, and came back for a few more loads. People brought their own containers to be filled straight from the vats: jugs, canning jars, five-gallon demijohns, beer kegs, 50-gallon barrels, milk cans, metal containers of all shapes and sizes with sometimes alarming provenance. With mixed emotions wineries obliged up to the midnight toll of Prohibition's doleful bell; midnight came later that night than usual.

If ever there was a hung-over morning-after, with grim consequences, it was the morning of January 21, 1920. In the quintessential wine town of Naples and its environs, every winery locked its doors except Widmer's. In and around Hammondsport all but four—Pleasant Valley, Taylor, Urbana, and Freidell—shut down operations. The venerable White Top Wine Company filed for dissolution, as did the Seneca Lake Wine Company. In the Chautauqua–Erie region, where most of the grape crop had already been channeled into juice operations, every winery announced it was closing except the little Fredonia Wine Co. Two wineries—Brotherhood and the Bolognesi's—stayed open in the Hudson Valley.

Those who continued to operate took advantage of a few regulatory doors left ajar. Permits could still be obtained to produce wine for religious sacraments, for medicinal use, for cooking and food processing (with salt added), for flavoring extracts, distilling into industrial-grade alcohol, and for beverages with their alcohol content reduced to 0.5 percent or less. An alphabet soup of 13 separate Permits A, H, K, L. etc. covered these various operations, tracked by rivers of paperwork overseen by both the Prohibition Administration and the Internal Revenue Service. Reports needed to be filed identifying the purchaser of every single sale. The prospect of dealing with all this in itself drove most winemakers out of the business. But those who persisted would be honed, by the very instruments meant to eviscerate them, into more nimble business machines, survivors with skills that would later carry the wine trade to new levels.

The amount of wine a resourceful producer could move through the door left open for sacramental wine, for example, proved extraordinary. The religious requirements for wine suddenly multiplied; churches began buying communion wine regularly by the barrel. There were no requirements for churches or synagogues to keep records or issue reports on the dispensation of sacramental wine, and federal agents were reluctant to look too closely at the goings-on within congregations. Storefront synagogues opened in New York City where anyone could walk in off the street, sign up with a rabbi behind the counter, and walk out with a case of household ceremonial wine.

The Pleasant Valley Wine Co. obtained a permit to make and sell sacramental wine, but PV made mostly sparkling wine and the Prohibition Administration ruled that sparklers did not fall within their definition of wine for sacraments. When PV threatened a lawsuit the administration relented, gave the winery a special exemption, and for a short time Pleasant Valley enjoyed the exclusive right to sell sparkling sacramental wine. When other wineries cried foul, a sympathetic judge in Washington finally put the matter to rest ruling "it is not the content of the beverage, but the purpose for which it will be used that determines whether or not it is a sacramental wine." This threw the door wide enough for wineries with the proper permit to begin selling not just sacramental champagne but sacramental port, sherry, and a complete selection of sacramental varietals, even sacramental brandy.

The same held true for medicinal wines, as long as the customer had a physician's prescription. A typical note came to the Pleasant Valley Wine Co. from a P. J. Flanigan in Ohio: "Dear Sirs, the doctor has recommended champagne for me. Please let me know if you will ship same and what price you have on Great Western Extra Dry." Anti-Prohibition physicians freely (and lucratively) dispensed prescriptions for medicinal wines, available at pharmacies. In 1922 the American Medical Association reversed its recent policy reversal on the medical value of wine; it now declared wine was in fact useful in treating no less than 27 different listed ailments (a 28th might have been the ailing state of doctors' own wine cellars).

So-called wine tonics could be sold without prescription. Concoctions of wine with various reputedly therapeutic ingredients (peptone, sodium of glycerophosphate) were able to evade the ban on "intoxicating liquors for beverage purposes"—these were not sold as beverages per se. Though they were poor stand-ins for a good dinner wine, still they sold well enough to move some inventory out of cellars. Widmer's offered a choice of port, sherry, or tokay wine tonics.

Widmer's was perhaps the best example of the agility and inventiveness that carried survivors through the Dry years. The company's Prohibition-era letterhead ticked off their product line, a grab-bag of the many things a company could do with grapes: altar wines, wine tonics, wine sauces, wine jellies, grape jellies, brandy jellies, grape syrups, grape pomace, medicinal wines, grape concentrates, dealcoholized wines, manufacturing wines, brandy sauces, manufacturing wine syrups, crème de menthe wine cordial dealcoholized. To promote some of these products Widmer's produced a musical radio program featuring a family with a cozy fondness for grapes: "At Home with the Schultzes."

Attempts to sell dealcoholized wine never came to much. Even the marketing clout of the Garrett Company could not persuade the public to abide Virginia Dare minus her alcohol; that effort fizzled. The most significant new wine market to open up during (and by virtue of) Prohibition was the meteoric rise of the home winemaker.

Hardly anyone foresaw the enthusiasm and the scale at which the American public would take to making wine at home, largely because no one had gauged the impact of a huge influx of wine-drinking immigrants in the preceding decades. For many of these folks, life without wine was unthinkable.

The Volstead Act allowed, by default, the legal production of wine in the home, primarily at the behest of the apple-growers' lobby to ensure that people could still make cider. This provided a new business angle for grape growers and wineries: marketing to the home winemaker. With 40 years of experience as a juice producer, The Taylor Wine Co.—now reviving its original name The Taylor Co.—made this its chief order of business. It began selling a line of "Wine Type" grape juices in 30-gallon casks with labels like Chablis and Burgundy. Each cask came with a packet of yeast and judiciously worded, detailed instructions on what not to do or wine would result. When Wine Types caught on, though Taylor had never made a champagne, they expanded the juice line to include sparkling cuvees and boldly offered the services of "specialists who will come direct from our cellars to your home and produce these sparkling types in your presence, by the same methods as used in the olden days."

Paul Garrett gave this end-run around Prohibition a higher profile with a nationally advertised product called Vine-Glo, distributed by a fleet of trucks: "Now is the time to order your supply of Vine-Glo. It can be made in your home in sixty days . . . in nine varieties: Port, Virginia Dare, Muscatel, Angelica, Tokay, Sauterne, Riesling, Claret and Burgundy. It is entirely legal in your home but it must not be transported." The Prohibition Administration disagreed and shut Vine-Glo down.

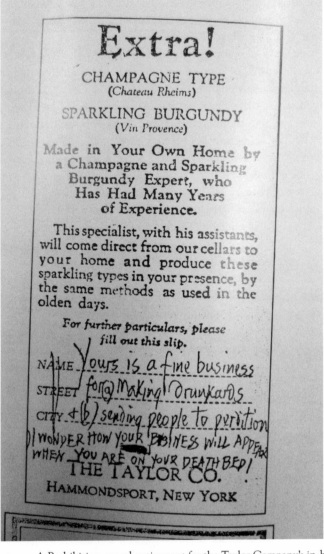

FIGURE 5.1. A Prohibition-era advertisement for the Taylor Company's in-home winemaking service managed to avoid using the word "wine." Wineries that stayed open through the dry years gingerly tested the limits of what the federal Prohibition Bureau would tolerate. This coupon was mailed back with a message filed away in Taylor's archive. (*Courtesy of the Glenn H. Curtiss Museum*)

During national Prohibition's first year New York was one of three states that attempted to defy the Volstead Act by passing legislation allowing the production of "light" (unfortified) wine and beer. The Supreme Court ruled it unconstitutional. In 1923 Governor Al Smith, a champion of "Wets," enthusiastically backed legislation that denied state funding for any enforcement of Prohibition. Section II of the 18th Amendment stated: "The Congress and the several States shall have concurrent power to enforce this article by appropriate legislation." States had the power to enforce and they could choose not to use it. Congress took a more nuanced approach. Its woefully inadequate budget for enforcement bedeviled Prohibition from the start. It was a classic case of politicians playing to both sides of a controversial issue; they could claim both the moral and fiscal high ground.

The 18th Amendment banned "the manufacture, sale, or transportation" of wine but not the storage of existing inventories, with, of course, the proper permit and bond. There were still more than 120 wineries bonded in the state of New York during the initial years of Prohibition, nearly all of them mothballed as winemaking operations but still sitting on cellars with many thousands of gallons of wine and brandy, waiting for the day the nation would come to its senses. The number would dwindle year by year as wines spoiled and owners lost hope. In the meantime they were inevitably the subjects of suspicion among federal agents.

Shortly after Prohibition took effect, a group of Brooklyn investors arranged to buy the shuttered Hammondsport Wine Co. with a down payment delivered as a wad of $5 and $100 bills. The company's assets included 3,000 cases of unfinished Golden Age Champagne, legally stored in tierage in the cellar. Some months later the Steuben County deputy sheriff, on his way to work one evening, noticed men milling around a truck at the company's loading dock. When federal agents arrived to investigate they discovered all but 300 cases of wine had disappeared; upon further investigation so had the company's new owners. The building was later sold at auction, purchased by none other than the same county deputy sheriff, who promptly resold it to the Hebrew National Sacramental Wine Company, a New York City-based operation that bought several Hammondsport wineries during the Prohibition years, selling off their inventories as sacramental wine.

The archives of the Prohibition Administration hold no record of illegal activities committed by those New York winemakers who held licenses to continue fermentation. They were either model law-abiding citizens or exceptionally clever clandestine operators. It is certainly true that most bootlegging involved hard liquor, but shady deals and wine busts like the night raid in Hammondsport did occasionally animate local newspapers. In February of 1921 agents stormed the basement of an old saloon in Syracuse. "The Armbruster café was one of the first to disappear before the dry tidal wave in this city," according to the *Syracuse Journal*, but "reports that the place was not as arid as it appeared reached prohibition headquarters a week or so ago." Eleven barrels of wine and hard cider were dumped in the street or confiscated, along with "an unusually large wine press." The following year the *New York Evening Telegram* reported 50,000 gallons of wine seized in a raid on the Spera & Martina Co., one of the Italian-immigrant wineries of Fredonia, "the largest seizure made in Chautauqua County."

In the heart of New York City the cellar of a Greenwich Village building was running full-tilt as a winery when federal agents burst in and chased the operators out the back door. They found 35 barrels of port and sherry, a wine press, and a stash of counterfeit wine withdrawal permits.

A raid at the Lake Erie region's Brocton Wine Cellars, officially closed, revealed a brandy pot—still churning out bootleg whiskey. That was a black eye for one of New York's venerable old-timers, but the state's highest-profile wine raid came down hard on the White Top Champagne Company, eight miles north of Hammondsport. It had shut down operations but still contained a storied inventory of top-of-the-line Keuka Lake sparkling wine, in legal storage. In November 1925, with festering suspicion but little provocation, the Steuben County sheriff's office again called in federal enforcement agents. They proceeded to ransack the White Top facilities, dumping 20,000 gallons of champagne into Keuka Lake. The Wheeler family owners chose to absorb the loss rather than take the government to court, but the county sheriff paid for his overreach with his job.

The scene was very different in nearby Naples, where the sheriff was nowhere to be seen, especially not on Rhine Street, named for the many German immigrants settling there during the late 1800s. In the recollection of one Naples resident, "on a Friday or Saturday night during the Prohibition era there was a steady stream of cars on Rhine Street to purchase the illegal but excellent 'homemade' Naples wines. In those days a gallon of wine sold for $2. Business was great and the Naples wine industry flourished illegally. As one reporter assessed the situation, 'you can't legislate good wine out of existence.'"

Local newspapers seemed to delight in recounting the many ways people maneuvered around the law. The Elmira paper described one such case:

A few days ago a truck driver visited Hammondsport with his truck, which had been filled with empty milk cans, and the truck started back to Elmira. The driver had partaken liberally in Hammondsport and on the return trip indulged frequently in wine from a convenient milk can. The result was he became drowsy and drove the truck alongside the highway where he stopped. Shortly after, a milk dealer driving a truck loaded with cans of milk became interested in the first truck and its driver, who unmindful of the cold was sleeping soundly in the seat. The milkman endeavored to arouse the truck driver, but without success, so he investigated and discovered the drowsy one was commanding a cargo of the stuff that cheers. Evidently the farmer does not mind a wee nip, when the occasion warrants, for he removed three cans of wine to his own truck and left three cans of milk in their place.

Wine was still flowing, but there was no doubt the industry as a whole was crippled. While liquor producers, through their bootlegging operations, got organized (criminally) into a powerful twentieth-century industry, wine producers got sidelined by home winemakers. And what about grape growers; how did they make out through the dry years? The sudden demand from home winemakers in the early days of Prohibition drove grape prices up from $40-per-ton wineries had been paying to $100 on the streets of New York City.

This naturally touched off a wave of vineyard planting. In New York it was a small wave: according to the U.S. Census of Agriculture, the state's vineyard acreage increased steadily but modestly from 1920 to 25 to 30. By contrast, California acreage—more than eight times New York's—shot up by 60 percent during the first five years of Prohibition. The ensuing flood of grapes glutted the market and prices plummeted. California dominated the market to home winemakers and New York growers suffered mightily from West Coast overplanting. While the size of New York's grape harvest was about the same in 1929 as in 1919, the crop lost two-thirds of its value. In the final years of Prohibition, Finger Lakes grapes sold for half what it cost to grow them. Many vineyards were abandoned.

Census figures for the state masked very different stories from region to region. Most of the vineyard planting during the 1920s took place in the Chautauqua–Erie grape belt, where Concord was king and grape juice processors were well-established; by the end of Prohibition 98 percent of the district's vineyards were planted to Concord. That easy-to-grow, prolific variety also dominated some planting done in the Finger Lakes while wine varieties like Delaware lost ground. The shift in the varietal mix toward Concord would have major implications for the future of New York wine. In the Hudson Valley, vineyard acreage continued a decline that had begun before the turn of the century.

Historians have come to disturbingly different conclusions about how national Prohibition changed America's drinking habits. In his 1998 book, *Battling Demon Rum: The Struggle for a Dry America*, Thomas Pegram asserts that Prohibition succeeded in reducing per capita alcohol consumption from 2.5 gallons in 1915 to less than one gallon in 1934. Daniel Okrent's *Last Call: The Rise and Fall of Prohibition* (2010) claims the amount of wine Americans drank *doubled* during Prohibition. A 1934 *Fortune Magazine* article said it *tripled*, and liquor consumption increased by 50 percent.

There were obviously no official reports on how much alcohol was made or sold illegally, and none also on how much was made in homes. The Prohibition era turned into a legal and illegal free-for-all that confounds attempts to measure its immediate effects on drinking, but a few conclusions seem safe. America was not what could be called a wine-drinking nation before Prohibition and it was not a wine-drinking nation after Repeal. Liquor and beer remained the chosen forms of alcohol; a period of desperation home-winemaking couldn't change that. The ubiquity of the sodden, male-fortress saloon, however, had been displaced by the speakeasy, where men and women danced and lightened-up together. Drinking had become more gender-neutral, more social. Women, who had battled against alcohol and for equal rights, came away with an ironic hybrid: a more egalitarian culture of alcohol.

The worst outcome of Prohibition was, of course, the rise of organized crime within the climate of a general disregard for the law. The high-profile horrors of street battles over control of the illegal liquor trade undermined any claims that Prohibition would be a stabilizing and beneficent force in society. The onset of the Great Depression evaporated another of the Drys' contentions, that Prohibition would energize the economy. Advocates for Repeal were now making the same claim. The Noble Experiment had become an ill-conceived distraction from more urgent matters. In the presidential campaign of 1931, Herbert Hoover kept pushing to enforce the 18th Amendment while Franklin Roosevelt, famously no teetotaler, let the issue work in his favor without speaking to it directly.

When Roosevelt swept the election, the fate of national Prohibition was sealed. The 21st Amendment to the Constitution, the first ever to annul an earlier amendment, won ratification even more rapidly than the 18th had, nearly 14 years earlier. The voting for Prohibition had been done by state legislatures. The voting for Repeal was done by state referenda. New Yorkers voted 8 to 1 for Repeal.

CHAPTER 6

Restart

I had no idea of the climate and the grapes I would have to work with. It was a sultry 100 degrees in the shade when I arrived in New York City. Then I tasted Concord, Catawba, Elvira and Isabella wines which, to say the least, gave me a shock . . . The winter that followed was the third shock! But as I had come under a one year contract, I stuck it out.

The wineries that endured Prohibition most-intact were those with the foresight and the initiative to prepare themselves for drought. It was no different 14 years later at Repeal: wineries anticipating and preparing for alcohol's return would soldier on with the best prospects.

Virtually all the wineries still alive managed to make more wine as the date of resurrection drew nearer, but two stood out. Widmer's Wine Cellars fermented more than 100,000 gallons in the fall of 1933, adding to a total of a third of a million gallons in inventory. In the years leading up to Repeal, The Taylor Company rejuvenated its coopering operation, assembling a battery of vats and barrels to stockpile nearly a million gallons.

Congress and the Bureau of Prohibition also made early adjustments. Six months before the 21st Amendment was approved, the bureau's budget for enforcement was slashed and half its agents let go.

When Utah became the 36th state to ratify, making Repeal the law of the land on December 5, 1933, the scene in Hammondsport was the mirror image of what it had been in January 1920: instead

91

of a horde of customers storming the cellars to stock up, the wineries unleashed an attack of wine upon the public. A special edition of the local paper described the final minutes on the front lines: "Dozens of trucks and private cars loaded at each one of the cellars and, released by Repeal, left with accelerators pressed to the floor to hasten the delivery of sparkling beverages to far distant points before midnight . . . Even airplanes were called into service as soon as they could legally take wing."

When the trucks and planes came back empty, reality settled in. Wine could flow again, the U.S. Constitution was repaired, but

FIGURE 6.1. A post-Prohibition ad for Great Western Champagne epitomized the social transformation during the "Noble Experiment." Compare this to the advertisement for Lake Erie Wine Cellars in chapter four. (*Courtesy of the Glenn H. Curtiss Museum*)

the prospect in nearly every direction was sobering. On the market side, in 1934 the nation was still mired in the deepest trough of the Great Depression; a quarter of the nation's workforce was unemployed and many of the rest were clinging to the edges of a listing economy. When the celebrations were over, where was the money or the appetite for wine?

Looking at the law, it became clear that the great leap of the Constitution, in and out of national Prohibition, had landed in a mudhole of state bureaucracies. When Congress confronted how to handle the return of alcohol, the matter was passed off to the individual states. Many chose to stay with statewide prohibition. Some loosened the reins on beer and wine while restricting the sale of spirits to tightly controlled liquor stores. New York—largely through the influence of upstate legislators from the once "burned-over district"—put in place high annual license fees, excise taxes and bonding requirements, bizarre price-posting regulations, and a three-tier distribution system that forced wineries to sell their products only to wholesale middlemen, guaranteeing higher prices down the line for the consumer without rewarding the producer. It was a regulatory maze that reinforced the trend toward large-scale businesses.

If it dared to look in the mirror, the industry saw much of its infrastructure in shambles. In the scores of wineries closed down during Prohibition, equipment lying idle for 14 years was rusted and derelict. Some of it had been sold to South American wineries or sold off for scrap. Empty cooperage dried out and warped. Any wine that had sat unattended in vats and barrels was often spoiled with vinegar organisms or worse, which compounded the loss by infecting the wood of valuable cooperage. Many winemakers and other personnel had drifted into other work.

On the supply side, things looked no better. The U.S. Census of Agriculture recorded a slump in New York vineyard acreage during the early 30s, reflecting the collapse of grape prices from overplanting in California. The figures only hint at what was happening on farms in the final years: half of New York's growers stopped spraying their vines; many vineyards were minimally maintained or essentially abandoned but still harvested (and counted by the census) as grapevines will continue giving at least some fruit through years of neglect. First to go were the vineyards on steeper slopes close to lake shores—older, harder to work, less productive, often the shyer-bearing varieties responsible for New York's best wines: Delaware, Iona, Dutchess, Diamond. They were key components of the sparkling wine cuvees that had been worked out over 50 years of experimentation.

Wineries were left with the output of vineyards dominated by Concord, a grape that shipped well, looked handsome in baskets, made the best juice and jelly but was useful to the winemaker primarily only for sweet, fortified sherries, port, tokay, or whatever label might be put on it. In that context Concord's flagrantly grapey aroma and flavor receded into something more generically marketable to alcohol-minded veterans of Prohibition. For better or worse, it would help New York wineries stumble through a very long, slow recovery. Rehabilitation of the state's primary, sparkling-wine tradition—the vineyards, the specialized equipment, the cellar skills—would take decades.

Along with Taylor and Widmer, the Garrett company emerged from Prohibition in reasonably good shape. Paul Garrett's various schemes—dealcoholized Virginia Dare, Vine-Glo concentrates for home winemakers, flavoring extracts, industrial alcohol, and others—hadn't always turned out well but the man was so irrepressibly inventive, such a strong presence in the industry and marketplace, he was able to revive America's only nationwide wine enterprise at least through the 1930s. Garrett & Co. quickly resumed wine sales in every wet state, averaging more than half a million gallons a year of Virginia Dare alone. Much of Garrett's attention now went to cooperative ventures in California and vineyard development in the South.

The Taylor Company's founder died a few months after Repeal, but Walter Taylor had already turned the business over to his three sons, Fred, Clarence, and Greyton. They had artfully marketed the "Wine-Types" juice that carried Taylor through the locust years. The brothers began signing long-term contracts with independent growers all over western New York.

The generations had turned over at Widmer's too. John Jacob retired in 1924 to spend his final years caring for his homestead vineyard, leaving winery affairs to his sons, Carl, Frank, and William, all three groomed for distinct roles in the business: Carl to manage company vineyards, Frank to run the business office, and Will to make the wine.

Will was the only Widmer child to graduate high school, after which, as he recalled later, "my father told me I was going to be a wine chemist and handed me a steamer ticket to Germany. I attended the Royal Academy of Wine Chemistry at Geisenheim on the Rhine . . . I also traveled all over Europe with a knapsack on my back and visited all the wine growing regions. My allowance was $75 a month. I really wanted to be an artist."

And he would be—in the cellar. During and following Prohibition Will Widmer gave his Naples wines a distinctly German accent, with a new awareness of yeast strains and late-harvest wine styles. He was the first Finger Lakes winemaker to recognize and explore the possibilities flowing from grapes infected with *edelfaule*, the botrytis mold looked upon by New York farmers as an affliction but responsible, as he'd learned, for Germany's most expensive wines.

Widmer's progressivism impressed Frank Schoonmaker, the most influential wine impresario in the years after Prohibition. Schoonmaker was an importer but also a great believer in the future of American wine, if American winemakers could only break some unfortunate habits. Chief among them, in his view, was the practice of giving European names like Burgundy and Rhine to American wines—disrespectful to both the originals and the impostors. He urged instead the use of American place names and grape varietal labels on wines made from single varieties. Widmer responded by delivering up a dozen post-Prohibition "Canandaigua Lake" varietals: Niagara, Iona, Elvira, Salem, Diana, Moore's Diamond, Delaware, Dutchess, Isabella, Vergennes, Catawba, and Riesling, all listing "A Frank Schoonmaker Selection" on neck labels. (The Riesling was in fact made from the native variety Missouri Riesling.) Widmer also vintage-dated the wines at a time when blending vintages was still common practice.

Most of the other wineries that persevered through Prohibition had done so clinging to the life-raft of sacramental wine, to come out in the end as haggard survivors. They might still have the ability to briefly punch up production for the flurry of demand at Repeal, but little else to show for the last 14 years and much to rebuild. Pleasant Valley and Urbana, the giants of American sparkling wine at the turn of the century, had been reduced to squabbling over the ersatz sacramental sparkling wine market. The venerable Brotherhood Wine

Company had limped along relying on tank-cars of California wine to replace disappearing Hudson Valley vineyards. In the valley only the Bolognesi family's Hudson Valley Wine Company came through in good shape, on the strength of close ties with the neighborhood's many monasteries.

There were also wineries—mainly larger operations—optimistically coming back to life after spending the drought years either shuttered or making jelly, candy, grape catsup, grape *something*. The Empire State Wine Company in Penn Yan, having survived on a diet of mostly jelly, mustered the capital to re-entered the sparkling wine business. The pioneer of the Chautauqua–Erie Grape Belt, Brocton Wine Cellars, reopened with a new owner from Boston, Jack Kaplan. He had made a fortune wheeling-and-dealing in molasses and thought he saw a chance to do the same with grapes. The Irondequoit Wine Company resumed operations outside Rochester. In Naples the Maxfield company stopped selling their grapes to Widmer's, resuscitated fermenters in the valley's oldest cellar, and started selling from an inventory that dated back to vintage 1901.

The Hammondsport Wine Company, scene of shenanigans during Prohibition, reopened in the hands of a dynamic local entrepreneur named Deyo W. Putnam. He had also acquired extensive vineyards on Bully Hill and grape-packing houses in town, where he sold fresh fruit and juice in the years before Repeal to the nation's largest food retailer, The Great Atlantic and Pacific Tea Company (A&P). In 1933 he brought back Golden Age Champagne and within three years the cellars of the old Hammondsport winery were filled with nearly two million gallons of wine. D. W. Putnam was a key figure in rebuilding the Keuka Lake wine scene. From his home at the top of Bully Hill his panorama of the lake included the lake-house of his colleague Paul Garrett on Bluff Point. With Garrett and the principals of the Taylor, Widmer, Pleasant Valley and Urbana wineries, Putnam formed the Finger Lakes Wine Association in 1932, a group that dominated the recovery of New York wine. When powerful interests in California attempted to insert into federal regulations a ban on adding sugar and water to wine musts, the Finger Lakes association lobbied successfully to block it.

Although the O-Neh-Da Winery had produced sacramental wine exclusively since 1872, it shut down during Prohibition; its Austrian winemaker was discovered to be in the country illegally and it couldn't compete with larger operations flooding the sacramental market. In 1934 the church hired a German emigrant named Leo Goering, trained at the same Geisenheim Institute Will Widmer had attended. He arrived on Hemlock Lake to find ten overgrown acres of vineyard and rows of handsome, chestnut vats filled with vinegar. On a shoestring church budget Goering slowly brought O-Neh-Da back to life.

Then there were the many wineries snuffed out by the 18th Amendment and never heard from again. Some had been major players. Seneca Lake's only winery, one of the region's most ambitious start-ups in the early days but plagued by fires and continually changing hands over the years, the Seneca Lake Wine Company was destroyed by fire one last time while idle in the mid-20s. White Top Cellars, originally the Crooked Lake Wine Company of 1870, ransacked by federal agents during Prohibition, never recovered. The Frey brothers' Germania Wine Cellars in Pleasant Valley, sold to a New York City investor in 1919 and moribund through most of Prohibition, did try briefly to come back but soon gave up.

More of the casualties were smaller, family-farm enterprises started by immigrants in the late 1800s, a generation dying off with either no heirs, none interested, or none able to carry on in disheartening times. Such was the fate of virtually all the "Italian" wineries in the Fredonia area; the entire community of winemakers in Dansville; the Graff, Rohlins, Dinzler, Miller, Katzenbach, Seeley, Fox, and Thrall wineries of the German enclave around Canandaigua Lake; all the wineries in Bath.

On Keuka Lake and around Hammondsport the list of the vanquished and vanished included The Vine City Wine Co., Haase's Rheims Wine Cellar, Connolly Brothers Winery, McCorn Wine Co., Funks Wine Co., Pulteney Wine Cellar, Eckel's Wine Cellar, Crescent Wine Co., D. Smutz Wine Co., Hammondsport Vintage Co., Cushing Wine Co., Foster Cellars, Lake View Wine Co., Rose Winery—each with its own story of a dream undone.

Even in the most disturbed and arid ground, some seeds will take root. On the Niagara River at Lewiston, near Niagara Falls, Chateau Gay opened its doors as a sparkling wine house—on its face a foolish choice when Americans were mostly buying fortified wines if they could afford anything—but the owners had an ace up their sleeve. A

French winemaker, Eugene Charmat, had recently designed equipment and procedures for making sparkling wine entirely in tanks, bypassing the traditional, slow, labor-intensive process of secondary fermentation in the bottle. A Canadian company bought the North American rights to Charmat's innovation, started using it in Ontario to make low-priced sparklers, and opened an American satellite across the river in Lewiston after Repeal. Chateau Gay introduced inexpensive, Depression-style champagne to the American market.

A Jewish cantor named Meyer Star and his son, Leo, found another market niche in nearby Chautauqua County. Meyer had emigrated in the 1890s from Poland to Pennsylvania, where he serviced small-town synagogues as both itinerant cantor and traveling salesman peddling kosher food and wine. Like Deacon Fay and Reverend Bostwick and others before him, he ran into the need for a local source of sacramental wine, and like them he decided to make his own. The Stars bought the Fredonia Wine Company during Prohibition. They were soon sending wine down to the "open synagogues" of New York City, but that ended when federal agents cracked down on the rampant sale of sacramental wine to bogus congregations.

The Stars's business genuinely took root after Repeal when Leo restarted the Fredonia facility and rented a double cellar on Manhattan's Wooster Street. There he bottled kosher Concord wine from Chautauqua mixed with tank-car wine from California. He called his Manhattan cellar the Monarch Wine Company. To the surprise of everyone including Star, his sweet, grapey wine quickly jumped from a specialty for Passover to a mass-market phenomenon. Even the baffling brand-name "Manischewitz," used under contract with a popular kosher foods company, didn't slow sales down; people asked for "that Massachusetts wine." Within a few years Monarch was operating out of huge facilities at Brooklyn's Bush Terminal industrial complex, also home to the East Coast hub of Garrett & Company.

Monarch was far from alone making kosher wine in the heart of the city after Prohibition. The Schapiro Wine Co. had been operating on the Lower East Side's Rivington Street since the turn of the century. A list of bonded wineries in New York State in 1934 included nearly a dozen located in New York City, almost all of them making some or all their wine kosher. One of them, Geffen Industries in Long Island

City, sold in bulk to bottlers up and down the East Coast. Geffen was run by Queens kingpin "Little Joe" Appelbaum, who reportedly made copious amounts of wine from relatively few tons of grapes, a skill learned by many in the school of Prohibition. Little Joe hired a small-time hustler named Mordecai "Mack" Sands as salesman, a gifted deal-maker who learned the ins and outs of the wine trade peddling Applebaum's wine from New England to the Carolinas. He would go on to style himself a sort of northern-Jewish Paul Garrett.

On a July morning in1935, rain began to fall in the Finger Lakes, intensifying over the next two days into the region's fiercest deluge of the century. Torrents roared through the glens and ravines that streaked the hills along the lakes, sometimes jumping out and ripping through vineyards that hard-pressed growers were struggling to nurse back to life. When it was over, at his farm near Valois on Seneca Lake, Elmer Porter could stand in the middle of his gullied vineyard, reach up and barely touch the bottom trellis wire. Keuka Lake had turned brown. In two days its surface level rose more than three feet.

Among the wine towns, Hammondsport was hardest hit. Glen Creek sliced through western hills directly into the heart of the village where the Roualet Winery, a converted watermill, perched on its bank. *The Keuka Grape Belt* newspaper described "an attack of flood waters" overrunning the building and its warehouse, flushing out 500 barrels of brandy and leaving them strewn through the village, snagged in uprooted trees and spiked along wrought-iron fences. Long sections of the Bath & Hammondsport Railroad tracks were washed out.

This spectacle must have dumped one more shock upon a young Frenchman recently arrived on Keuka Lake to take charge of one of its grand institutions. The Urbana Wine Company had come under the ownership of the Underhill family during Prohibition, local descendants of the same Underhills who planted the Hudson Valley's first commercial vineyard at Croton Point a century earlier. Urbana had an unbroken line of winemakers from the French Champagne district since its first vintage in 1865. After Repeal, winery president Eugene Underhill Jr. naturally turned to France again for help restoring a great sparkling-wine house lately down on its luck. He asked Charles Fournier, production manager of one of Champagne's most prestigious firms, Veuve Clicquot Ponsardin, for a recommendation.

FIGURE 6.2. Hammondsport's town square was covered with debris and barrels flushed out of the Roualet winery by the 1935 flood—one more blow to an industry on its knees after Prohibition. Hundreds of barrels littered the streets of the village. Roualet never reopened, though its massive edifice, once the largest freestanding stone buildings in the state after the capitol, stood empty at the edge of town into the 21ˢᵗ century. (*Courtesy of the Steuben County Historical Society*)

The 32-year-old Fournier was just emerging from a failed marriage and feeling unmoored. He had been groomed to take over as wine master at Veuve Clicquot by his uncle who, with the rest of the Champenois community, surely found it *incroyable* when the young man agreed to take the Urbana job himself, for one year. Underhill had no doubt ticked off the names of his past winemakers—Charles LeBreton from Roederer, Jules Crance from Moet et Chandon—but he apparently neglected to mention details about Finger Lakes winegrowing. "I had no idea," Fournier later recalled, "of the climate and the grapes I would have to work with. It was a sultry 100 degrees in the shade when I arrived in New York City. Then I tasted Concord, Catawba, Elvira and Isabella wines which, to say the least, gave me a shock. In addition, the winemaking science there was very limited. The winter that followed was the third shock! But as I had come under a one year contract, I stuck it out."

With the 1934 vintage he immediately set about lightening up Urbana's wine style, drawing down the use of brandy and sugar and experimenting with ways to refine native grape flavors. He had brought with him from Veuve Clicquot his own Champagne yeast culture. When his one-year contract ended, the work had barely begun. He chose to stay on.

Fournier heard from all directions that growing the grape varieties familiar to him in Champagne was commercially impossible on Keuka Lake. The Geneva Experiment Station still viewed European vinifera grapes as exotics for backyard wine enthusiasts motivated to bury their vines each winter. Fournier was also familiar, however, with hybrids of French and American grape varieties that had been developed by French plant breeders responding to the European phylloxera vineyard epidemic of the late 1800s. The *raison d'etre* of the hybrids was the combination, in stricken French vineyards, of North American hardiness with European finesse. Why not apply the same logic to the slopes of Keuka Lake? In the spring of 1936 Urbana put a test planting behind the winery of the hybrids Seibel 1000 and Ravat 6, named after their breeders.

Those vines may have come directly from France or from the Geneva Experiment Station, where French hybrids had been growing in research and breeding blocks since shortly after the turn of the century. The station's Professor Richard Wellington took a particular interest in the hybrids coming out of France. In the early 1920s he supplied vines to Charles Champlin, Jr. for an experimental planting on the slope behind the Pleasant Valley Wine Company, the first American test of French hybrids by a commercial winery. Although the timing of a wine-grape trial at the outset of Prohibition was unfortunate, it went well enough for Champlin to convince at least one PV grower-supplier, Harry Longwell, to add five acres of Seibel 1000 to his vineyard north of Hammondsport. Longwell's vines can fairly be called the first commercial-scale plot of a French hybrid variety grown outside Europe.

Starting in the late 1930s a small group of winegrowers and researchers began to meet occasionally, unofficially, in Geneva or at the experiment station's satellite research facility in Fredonia to study the hybrids, share bits of experience and taste experimental wines. The group included Wellington, Fournier, Geneva researchers John Einset and Willard Robinson, Canadian winemakers Aldemar deChaunac and George Hostetter, and Maryland newspaperman Philip Wagner, an avid amateur winegrower who had discovered the hybrids in Europe as a foreign correspondent. In the late 30s, just as this influential group of men was recognizing the revolution these new grape varieties might bring to New York and eastern American wine, the war in Europe closed off the supply of vines.

A wounded and disheveled wine industry suffered through the years of Depression, then struggled with wartime shortages of equipment, rationing of critical supplies like sugar and fuel, burdensome price controls, and the diversion of grape crops to provide massive quantities of juice for the military. For every winemaker successfully finding a foothold in this difficult landscape, there were at least as many unable to go on, among them sadly more of the pioneers: Brocton Wine Cellars on Lake Erie, the Irondequoit Wine Company on Lake Ontario, and in Naples the Maxfield winery, taken over in 1941 by its old rival Widmer's. Recovery from the setback of Prohibition did not fully take hold in the New York wine industry or the rest of the country until after World War II.

There were, in the meantime, stirrings in the vineyards that would lead to big changes in New York wine. The few tentative plots of French hybrids were full of promise. The revolution that would bring vinifera wines into commercial production was still at least a decade off but there were a few tantalizing hints it was coming. An American Wine and Food Society tasting at New York's Ritz-Carlton Hotel in February 1941, orchestrated by Frank Schoonmaker & Company, included a Canandaigua Lake Riesling. The event notes read "Mr. Widmer succeeded in harvesting a small, experimental patch of true Riesling vines in the fall of 1939 and producing this extraordinary wine, of which no commercial quantities exist"; still experimental, but a Finger Lakes Riesling floated into the ether of New York City public relations.

There was a great need for vineyard replanting to be done in the 1930s, but not much ability. New York's grape acreage continued to decline from 1930 to 1945, by 10 percent in the Finger Lakes, 45 percent in the rest of the state. Vineyard conditions and practices had not changed significantly for 50 years. Tractors were just beginning to take over some farming jobs from horses, but the side-hills of lake-hugging vineyards were too steep for machines. The transition from horsepower to tractors in vineyards extended well into the 1960s.

A new generation of commercial pesticides also appeared in the 1930s and 40s. At that time growers were still mixing up their own preparations from a handful of basic inorganic compounds: sulfur, lime, copper sulfate, lead powder, arsenic. Sulfur was first dusted on grapevines with bellows in the 1820s to discourage mildew. When the French concoction of copper sulfate and lime, Bordeaux mixture, was first tried in New York vineyards in 1889—a soggy season across the state—farm journals vibrated with accounts of crops brought back from the brink of ruin. Arsenate of lead came into use around the same time, as an insecticide spray, displacing difficult applications of nicotine with tobacco smoke.

All of these materials were hard on vines and harder still on farmers and horses. They were routinely used at high rates with little awareness or concern about worker exposure and health risks. And they hardly guaranteed abundant crops; the average yield per acre in New York vineyards post-Prohibition was one-and-a-half to two tons, essentially unchanged for nearly a hundred years.

A new class of synthetic, petroleum-based pesticides evolved from experiments developing agents of chemical warfare in Nazi-Germany. The first herbicides also came out of these laboratories of toxicology. They gave rise to an agrichemical industry. When DDT became available, the Geneva Experiment Station cautioned growers about potential dangers, but the impact this new generation of sprays had on vine-disease control and crop yields was dramatic and irresistible.

Another change, small but revealing in its own way, involved how growers tied their vines to the trellis. There were two times each year when grapevines required tying, first in early spring when the branches left after pruning needed to be secured to wires for support. This coincided with the time when willow trees growing along hedgerow creeks sent out new growth, and grape farmers used these sinewy-green shoots for vine ties, with a special gentle knot. They called it "willowing the vines." Later in summer when vines started to sprawl they were tied up again, the "straw tying," using stems of rye-grass. Every grape farm planted a patch of rye timed so the stems were long and supple just when grapevines needed coiffing.

That was how things had always been done. But in the new era of tractors and synthetic pesticides all this partnering with the rhythms of nature began to seem quaint and tedious, easily replaced with a box of jute twine or wire twists.

During World War II the German heritage of wine culture around the south end of Canandaigua Lake added an odd chapter to that area's wine history. Many young cellar workers were away in the military, leaving wineries short-handed. Will Widmer, fluent in German and always the innovator, contracted with the U.S. War Department to establish a branch prisoner-of-war camp at the winery compound. In 1944 almost 800 German POWs and guards traveled from Fort Niagara to Naples, where many spent the rest of the war as vineyard workers and cellar-rats making Widmer wine.

After the war, with the nation liberated from wartime constrictions and looking toward an era of prosperity, New York's wine industry began coming back to a life increasingly overseen by four Finger Lakes families: the Taylors, Widmers, the Champlins of Pleasant Valley, and the Underhills of Urbana.

Widmer's promoted their line of varietal wines but production at all these wineries and nearly all the others around the state concentrated on their well-established catalogues of fortified wines and sparklers. The experience of Prohibition had raised the ante in the American public's taste for alcohol in wine. Wines pumped up with brandy accounted for over half of postwar production from New York to California.

Sparkling wine, on the other hand, had always been New York's unique strength and claim to fame. The surviving sparkling wine houses of Keuka Lake—Pleasant Valley, Urbana, Empire State, D. W. Putnam's Hammondsport Wine Company—worked together to reassert the lake's reputation as the font of American champagne. The Taylor Wine Company never made sparkling wine before Prohibition but the brothers Taylor had stormed into the champagne market in 1936 and rapidly became the region's major producer. During the decade of the 1940s Charles Fournier added wine from French hybrid grapes into the cuvee for Urbana's flagship sparkler, Gold Seal Blanc de Blancs. That wine won the only gold medal awarded to an American sparkling wine at the California State Fair of 1950, the first and last year the judging accepted entries from out of state.

The end of the war—and even before that—the liberation of France, opened the door for importing more French hybrid planting material to the United States, including newer more promising varieties. Urbana and Widmer's planted their first large-scale French hybrid vineyards in 1944. The Taylor winery soon followed, characteristically in a bigger way. In 1943 Taylor had acquired the Longwell farm with its five acres of hybrid vines already producing a full crop. Will Widmer predictably put the first varietal hybrid wine on the market, a 1949 Seibel Rose. It was for many years an anomaly; French hybrids were initially used, like California tank-car wine, to soft-pedal native-grape flavors in generic blends

The wineries were working informally with experiment station researchers like Wellington and Robinson, but the official position of the station was still hamstrung by neo-Prohibitionist restrictions. While there had been a brief interlude of federally funded wine research in the late 30s, the state legislature continued to veto money for wine. As late as 1953, when wineries and growers were planting hundreds of acres of French hybrid wine grapes, the station's extension bulletin barely mentioned one Seibel variety at the end of a long list of recommended American grapes.

The Geneva Experiment Station hired its first full-time viticulturist, working exclusively with grapes, in 1944: Nelson Shaulis. One of his first major research projects put a 43-acre vineyard where no farmer worth his dirt would have considered planting grapes: on the boggy flats dribbling off Canandaigua Lake's south end. The plan was to test a site that might achieve higher crop yields through, counterintuitively, irrigation.

Tradition and common sense dictated that vineyards occupy hillsides where water and cold air drained away; never in lowland sinks. Shaulis wisely pitched his hair-brained scheme to innovator Will Widmer. The site was first cross-hatched with drainage ditches to lower the water table, then underscored with a grid of sub-irrigation pipes connected to lake water, for precise control of moisture to the vines. Irrigation had never been used in Finger Lakes vineyards. Bigger crops, Shaulis theorized, would compensate for an occasional loss from spring frosts and winter freezes.

Neighboring hillside vineyards served as controls. In the first cropping year the flats vines produced a stunning seven tons per acre; the hillside, a regionally typical two tons. The following year the flats experienced an equally stunning total crop loss from late-spring frost, while the control delivered a normal two-ton yield. Over the next five years Shaulis's theory and Widmer's gamble paid off: the irrigated vines averaged a crop four times bigger—the highest yields of any vineyard east of California.

Widmer's went on to plant more of the Naples Valley flats, but the project did not change the terrain of Finger Lakes viticulture or lead to routine irrigation. It was significant instead as an introduction to the man who would direct experiment-station research and outreach for the next four decades, and in that capacity exert great influence—analytical, yield-driven, focused on native American varieties—over New York viniculture during its time of recovery.

The family of Pleasant Valley Wine Company founder Charles Champlin ran that Finger Lakes original for nearly a full century. His grandson Charles D. Champlin II was winery manager when he died in 1950. Five years later the company passed into the hands of a New Jersey investor, signaling the start of potent changes in ownership of the New York wine industry. Old family ties to cellars and vineyards were beginning to unravel.

It was happening at the Urbana Wine Company. In 1957, company accountant Paul Schlem engineered a liaison with California's Almaden Vineyards, an ill-fated pairing that ended two years later when Schlem, his cousin Arthur Brody, and other New York City investors bought the company and renamed it Gold Seal Vineyards after its famous sparkling wine brand. Charles Fournier stayed on as president but Schlem and Brody took the reins.

By the late 1950s Taylor had become the dominant player in Finger Lakes wine and the largest American winery outside California. The three brothers applied their various skills with great success: Fred a natural-born salesman, Clarence the detail operations man, Greyton the visionary. Within several years of entering the champagne market they were making more sparkling wine than any other American winery. Greyton oversaw the region's most ambitious planting of the new French hybrids, singling out the Seibel variety rechristened Aurore. Supplementing their own hundreds of vineyard acres draped over Bully Hill and beyond, the company cultivated a region-wide network of contract growers, many of them old family friends working thousands of acres of grapes. By the end of the 1950s annual wine sales approached 2.5 million gallons.

"They are the pacesetters . . ." Philip Wagner wrote admiringly of the Taylors around 1960, "the pacesetters on wages . . . on prices paid for grapes to independent growers and on premium payments for superior quality . . . in assuming a large share of the chanciness in grape growing by buying vineyards and installing the former owners of them, as employees on salary, in their own homes . . . pacesetters in applying modern processing techniques."

In their book *American Wines*, Frank Schoonmaker and Tom Marvel described the same scene differently: "Wine producing has developed along the lines of a sort of modified feudal system, with the bonded winery as the baronial seat and the grape farmers in the surrounding neighborhood as the serfs."

The wine cellars of Taylor and Pleasant Valley were separated by a narrow driveway. When shares of stock in PV became available in 1961, Taylor leaped at the chance to buy a controlling interest in their august neighbor. To afford the deal, the family surrendered sole company ownership with a public stock offering, bringing investors into the management loop.

In the same year Taylor went public, the Widmer family sold out to Rochester financiers, who promptly installed corporate manager and marketing wizard Ernest Reveal as president. True to his name, he laid out the new ground rules: "Winemaking is going to be a big business in this country and as such will be run by big business."

Business Week magazine summed up what was happening in the Finger Lakes and elsewhere in the state with an article entitled *New York's Vintners Take a Bigger Sip*:

> There is a new genius in the vineyard—the professional manager. These men began to appear in the late 1950s as the combined task of making wine, mastering the complexities of marketing, and providing the capital for expansion proved too much for the resources of the family-owned wineries.

CHAPTER 7

Revolutionaries

As New York's wine industry consolidated through the 1950s and '60s, a small number of strong personalities came on the scene challenging the corporate paradigm. They mapped out a tumultuous reformation of winegrowing across the state.

Everett S. Crosby (1911–94)

Everett Crosby came of age in upper-middle-class California during Prohibition, and it was in fact Prohibition—he called it "the golden age of Prohibition"—that headed him into a career in wine. Anything prohibited was, to his teenage sensibility, by definition something to be desired. Beyond that, in Alameda County on the edge of vineyard country, wine was easy enough to be had—at any age. It was no more illegal for a bootlegger to sell to a 15-year-old than to a 50-year-old. Hence Crosby's introduction to wine in the rumble seat of a roadster after high school basketball games.

When he was still in high school Crosby's parents sent him off to Europe for a summer, where he learned that wine could be more than a good time after the game. It was the first of many trips through European vineyards. After college in 1935 he moved to New York City in pursuit of a singing career, drifted into acting and theater, and eventually found his footing as a script writer for radio. He worked for the Voice of America during World War II. Afterward he wrote Dick Tracy radio dramas and dabbled in early television. On the terrace of their Manhattan penthouse apartment he and his wife Alma sampled viticulture with a couple of Concord vines growing in butter tubs.

What could one do to pursue winegrowing in the 1940s land of Concord? The beginnings of an answer came at a favorite local Viennese restaurant that offered wines from Widmer's Cellars in the Finger Lakes. The Crosbys were struck by Widmer's varietal whites, made from native American grape varieties but with a brisk, European freshness and delicacy. (At the time, California wine master Louis Martini called Will Widmer the best maker of white wine in America.)

The Widmer example prompted Crosby to try his hand at making New York wine. He bought property near the Hudson River at West Nyack and planted a patch of vines in a soggy field that would deliver his first, painful, years-long lesson in grape culture. Only then did he read the current textbook on eastern American grape-growing, Philip Wagner's *A Wine-Grower's Guide*. Wagner had started experimenting with French hybrid wine varieties at his Maryland home in the early 1940s, wrote his landmark guide, started selling vines and, in 1945, opened a small winery: Boordy Vineyards. It became Everett Crosby's model.

In 1950 he purchased 78 acres on the eastern shoulder of a promontory near Nyack called High Tor, a landmark recently made famous by a Sherwood Anderson play of the same name. The property was rocky, well-drained, encrusted in woods, about a mile west of the river and Croton Point. Crosby was 39 years old. He had never been on a tractor. He ordered 3,500 French hybrid grapevines from the Boordy Nursery and left it up to Philip Wagner to decide which varieties to send. The vines launched High Tor Vineyards in 1951: they were still just numbered varieties at the time, later named Aurore, Seyval Blanc, Baco Noir. It was the first wine estate in New York planted exclusively to French hybrid grapes.

A concrete-block winery went up the following year and with vintage 1953 New York State had its first small, farm-based winery since Prohibition, in Rockland County 20 miles north of the George Washington Bridge. The labels simply said Rockland White and Rockland Red. Like Wagner, Crosby's intention was not to compete with the best of Europe but simply to make a good local wine and make it inexpensive.

As the vineyard came into full production and more vines went in, the new winery acquired one of the first Willmes bladder presses imported into the United States from Germany, a new design using pneumatic pressure to gently extract clearer juice. In the early years Crosby tended the vineyard and made the wine on his own. He learned the craft on the job, from books, and on visits to Widmer's and Boordy and European cellars. He made dry wine that reminded a prominent New York City merchant of "a big Loire." High Tor ran utterly against the tide of sweet, fortified wines coming out of consolidating, industrializing operations in New York and California, and it captured the fancy of high-end Manhattan wine shops tickled to receive deliveries by Crosby himself in his Oldsmobile station wagon. He was the prototype of many an urbane, untrained, small-scale New York winegrower to come.

The vineyard grew to 12 acres, though wine production never went much above 1,000 cases a year from a stingy crop of less than two tons to the acre. Crosby experimented successfully with Riesling but chose not to take that road. In the cellar he prided himself on rejecting the stew of chemicals, additives, and enzymes routinely used in the industry: "[T]here are a few who believe that wine is the product of the juice of sound, ripe grapes, period. I am one of those." He was determined to make "pure" wines but he was not a purist. During the first several years he occasionally bought barrels of California wine for blending and stretching small crops.

As such an odd little fish swimming upstream, High Tor ran directly into the nets of government regulators, taxmen, and assorted bureaucrats accustomed to dealing with corporate managers and accounting departments. In his memoir, *The Vintage Years*, Crosby rails about his chronic run-ins with

> the most insane set of strictures and regulations ever
> thought up by the mind of man. And their interference is
> in inverse ratio to the size of the winemaking operation.
> If you are a giant you will have clerks and secretaries who
> do nothing but thread their daily ways through the maze
> of regulations . . . you will have computers programmed
> to anticipate the next bureaucratic idiocy . . . If, however,

you are High Tor Vineyards, you are clerk, secretary, plant foreman, vineyard manager and computer rolled into one harried person . . . everything else grinds to a halt.

By the late 1960s suburbanization was spreading around High Tor and developers came knocking. The Crosbys began to tire of the demands and the workload, hired more help and spent more time at their hideaway in the Caribbean. They had never been financially reliant on the business; a good thing, as it never made much money. Too often the hired help made a mess of things. In the end, parts of the vineyard were abandoned and wine production withered.

Crosby sold his dream in 1971 to a High Tor admirer and entrepreneur named Richard Voigt. The business struggled on for a few years under the stewardship of winemaker Thomas Hayes, a restless Episcopal minister looking for a dream of his own, but it was too late. The equipment was sold off and the vineyard surrendered to real estate developers in 1976. High Tor had kindled a new movement in New York wine, but its own time had come and gone.

Frederick S. Johnson (1921–98)

The location of Johnson Estate Winery, on the Lake Erie escarpment, was originally the choice of someone who had his pick of the entire, pristine landscape of Chautauqua and Cattaraugus Counties. William Peacock surveyed that territory in the very early 1800s for the Holland Land Company and selected a site on Freelings Creek to clear for his own farm, above what would become the village of Westfield. His descendants planted fruit trees and grapes.

The Peacock family sold their farm to an English-born Canadian immigrant named Frederick W. Johnson in 1911. With a degree in entomology from Cornell, he worked for the U.S. Department of Agriculture as he built up a fruit business he called "Sunnyslope," selling to the juice and table markets. In 1920 he disassembled an 1800 dairy barn for timbers to frame an apple cold-storage building that would ultimately become the estate winery. During Prohibition his young son watched him make wine in the farmhouse cellar.

Fred Jr. (Frederick S.) followed his father to Cornell, studied horticulture and chemistry, and landed a job with Dole Pineapple in Hawaii that led to a career managing corporate agricultural plantations in Central America, Africa and Spain. He was supervising Nelson Rockefeller properties in Venezuela and Ecuador when word came in 1960 that his father had died.

Sunnyslope had suffered during turmoil in the grape market after World War II and through Frederick Sr.'s declining years. Young Fred returned home with plans to insulate the 125-acre farm from market volatility and put it on a self-sufficient track by making wine. He had come to know the wines of many celebrated regions in his travels and decided there was no reason why Chautauqua couldn't join them making something more interesting than grape juice and kosher Concord.

Most of the old orchards and Concord vineyards were cleared out and, in consultation with Nelson Shaulis at Cornell, Johnson replanted the farm with some of the region's first French hybrid grapes along with his favorite natives, Delaware and Ives. The reconfigured cold-storage barn started producing Johnson Estate wine in 1961. Mindful of the Chautauqua area's teetotaling history, Johnson introduced his own wine label in a quiet way at first, selling most of his production in bulk to Taylor. He was breaking ground to reclaim the nineteenth-century winemaking legacy of Elijah Fay and Garrett Ryckman.

The financial resources and business acumen Fred Johnson brought to the farm from his years abroad, combined with Sunnyslope's exceptional site, gave Johnson Estate a solid start. Production steadily increased through the 60s. The vineyard picked up more hybrid varieties but Delaware and Ives continued to anchor the list of wines. Johnson was creating a model for the resurgence of the Chautauqua–Erie grape belt as a wine district. He would stand at Governor Hugh Carey'a side when Carey signed the state's landmark Farm Winery Law.

Konstantin Frank (1899–1985)

In 1953 Charles Fournier, recently named president of the Urbana Wine Company, attended a conference at the New York State Agricultural Experiment Station in Geneva. During a break between sessions he was accosted, in French, by an agitated little man who grabbed him by the lapel, demanding to know why Urbana did not make wine from vinifera grapes.

This was Konstantin Frank, a field worker on the station's research farm. He was 54 years old with a surprising story behind him. Frank's grandfather was part of a group of Alsatian Germans invited to the southern Ukraine region of Russia in the early 1800s to import Western agricultural expertise, including viticulture. The German immigrants maintained their cultural identity in insular communities, into one of which Konstantin was born in 1899. He worked in his father's vineyard from the age of 12 and studied viticulture at the Odessa Polytechnic Institute off and on during the tumultuous years of the Russian Revolution.

Eventually a member of the institute's faculty with a doctorate in agricultural science (his dissertation was entitled "Studies in the Prevention of Winter Freeze Damage to the Grape"), Frank was assigned by the state to rehabilitate a 2,000-acre vineyard planted decades earlier and now ravaged by phylloxera. It was replanted successfully with vinifera vines grafted to American rootstocks, an undertaking he later credited with teaching him how to grow grapes. During the 1930s, supervising the gigantic collective farm, Comrade Frank invented plows to cover and uncover vines for protection from the bitter cold of the Ukrainian winter, a job previously done by 800 men with shovels and hoes.

When the Nazi army invaded Russia in 1941, the German communities welcomed them. When the Russian army drove the Nazis out, Frank fled with his young family back to German territory. He managed farms in Austria and Bavaria through the war's end and the allied occupation, finally managing to emigrate to America in 1951.

He arrived in New York City with his wife, three children, his library of 50 French books on viticulture and enology, virtually no money, and no knowledge of English, though he spoke fluent French and Russian as well as German. He washed dishes at a Horn & Hardart automat until he could afford a one-way ticket to the nearest agricultural research center, at Geneva, leaving his family behind until later.

At the Odessa Institute Frank had a large staff and his own personal chauffeur. At the New York Experiment Station, as one of five foreign scientists hired that year, he was addressed as Dr. Frank but expected, like other staff, to put time in on fieldwork including, to his enduring consternation, hoeing blueberries. He also worked with station viticulturist Nelson Shaulis monitoring trials on Concord grapes and vainly trying, in primitive English, to convince Shaulis they should be working with European grapes. The two men—both brilliant researchers, intense, in their own ways blindered—would feud for the rest of their lives. A year later Frank found, in the hallway outside a conference, someone who would listen to his preposterous claims about growing vinifera grapevines in a climate colder than the Finger Lakes'—"where spit freeze before hit ground."

The inquisitive, urbane Fournier and the pugnacious, obsessed Frank became lifelong or at least half-lifelong friends, both being in their fifties. Fournier had been dissuaded from even attempting to grow vinifera by the Experiment Station brain trust. He was intrigued by Frank's credentials and absolute certainty that it could be done. He was also no doubt aware of an experiment already well underway 100 miles northwest of the Finger Lakes on the Canadian Niagara Peninsula, at Brights Wine Company. There Fournier's friend and fellow French émigré Aldemar deChaunac, with his vineyard director George Hostetter, had begun experimenting with vinifera grapevines as early as 1946 and by 1951 had 10 acres planted in Chardonnay.

Soon after they met, Fournier hired Frank to direct vineyard research at Urbana, later renamed the Gold Seal Wine Company. Together they launched into an intensive research effort centered on the hill behind the old winery but taking them as far as Quebec, visiting a French-Canadian monastery garden in Fournier's Alfa-Romeo in search of native rootstock vines with maximum cold hardiness. They gathered European-variety scion material from the 50-year-old collection at the Geneva station and from research stations in Germany, California, and Russia.

Although in the Ukraine Frank buried vines for the winter, he had become convinced, in the milder climate of New York, that the selection of proper rootstocks could carry vinifera through the winters. The need to bury vines had been the major impediment to bringing vinifera grape culture from the experimental into the commercial sphere. The challenge Frank saw was to find rootstocks that would strengthen the vine, modulate its growth between the extremes of too weak and too vigorous, and expedite the ripening of both fruit and vine tissue. This was European thinking; at the Geneva station Shaulis and his colleagues discounted the influence of rootstocks and still held that vinifera was too commercially risky.

In the next half dozen years Konstantin Frank personally grafted over a quarter of a million grapevines in thousands of combinations of 58 different rootstocks with 12 vinifera varieties planted in nine different soil types. There were many dead ends, but the successes produced a bumper crop in 1957, after the test of a particularly severe winter. Experimental batches of wine from that vintage convinced Gold Seal to begin larger-scale planting of Riesling, Chardonnay, and Pinot Noir. The first limited commercial release of those varietals came with vintage 1959; the first substantial release in 1960.

To the vindicated and triumphant Dr. Frank, it now seemed obvious that Gold Seal would rip out its native-grape and French hybrid vineyards and replant with vinifera. His was an all-or-nothing world. The company hierarchy, including Charles Fournier, did not agree. A very popular Pink Catawba was Gold Seal's bread-and-butter product at the time and the commitment to French hybrids was in full force. Frank's demands for the primacy of his vinifera project escalated into personal conflicts. "The happy result," as Gold Seal vice-president Alex Brailow later put it, "is Vinifera Wine Cellars"—Frank off on his own with his pointedly named wine estate.

As early as 1956 Frank had saved enough money for a down payment on a 118-acre farm up-slope from Gold Seal, property once part of the pre-Prohibition Western New York Wine Company. Frank was grafting vines for his own farm as he cranked out vines for Gold Seal. He eventually put in more than 60 different vinifera wine and table grape varieties on his property (where he also continued to grow native American grapes for Gold Seal and for rootstock). From the beginning his efforts were all about both experimentation *and* evangelism. Every vinifera vine in his 70-acre vineyard was numbered and tracked in his field journal. At the same time he began selling juice and vines and dispensing advice, expertise, and opinion, without charge, to anyone who would listen. Many did; his front porch became a mecca for European-style wine aficionados, convocations that gave birth to the American Wine Society. His vineyard and cellar became a place for aspiring winegrowers to work a harvest and crush, perhaps to become one of what he called his "cooperators." They would be pioneers of vinifera winegrowing throughout the East, from Virginia to Arkansas to Massachusetts.

Figure 7.1. Konstantin Frank in the 1960s, with a basket of his precious vinifera grapes, and his wife Eugenie, an unsung supporting-player in the revolution taking place in eastern American wine. Once he left Gold Seal to start his own vineyard, nursery, and wine business, Frank attracted followers who became his network of "cooperators" in the spread of vinifera grape culture around the eastern U.S. His example inspired local winegrowers but his cooperators tended to be farther afield; Frank liked being center-stage in the Finger Lakes. (*Courtesy of the Steuben County Historical Society*)

Frank left his position at Gold Seal in 1961 and threw all of his still remarkable energy, at age 62, into his Vinifera Wine Cellars. The first result was a 1962 Johannisberg Riesling. Freed from whatever reticence he may have felt working side-by-side with his friend and patron Fournier, he now let loose the full force of his convictions: viniferas *must be the* wines of eastern as well as western America; native grapes made "junk;" French hybrids were worse than junk, they were toxic. For this strange claim he cited an obscure Romanian research trial where chickens fed a diet of hybrid grapes produced malformed chicks. The research was widely discredited (they were malnourished) but Frank latched onto it with his usual tenacity, calling up the chickens to warn winery visitors about risks of kidney and liver damage and birth defects. When syndicated columnist Jack Anderson gave Frank's rant a national audience, the New York wine establishment went on red alert. Nelson Shaulis reportedly called Frank "worse than phylloxera!" Philip Wagner, who had devoted the last 30 years to promoting French hybrid wine, tempered his exasperation with the detachment of a journalist: "I never cease to marvel that anyone could be so totally sure of himself and scornful of the slightest disagreement."

Frank's relations with the industry had always been stormy; even with the phlegmatic Fournier there were passing squalls. In his own bull-headed way he was showing considerable skill at public relations and political lobbying. Personal appeals by an emissary from the New York State Wine Growers Association to quiet him down went nowhere. Fournier shrugged it all off.

In the course of the 1960s Vinifera Wine Cellars became a critical hit, riding on its breakthrough in New York viticulture. The quality of the wines—Riesling, Chardonnay, Pinot Noir, Aligote, Gewurztraminer—was uneven: at best they were the peers of fancy Europeans standing next to them on store shelves and restaurant lists; at their worst they provided over-oaked, oxidized ammunition for the naysayers. The critiques had more to do with winemaking than with good grapes; Frank was primarily a viticulturist. Still his Riesling, in particular, rose into the realm of governor's-mansion accolades and White House dinners. New York wine had not caused such excitement since the glory days of nineteenth-century Keuka Lake champagne.

Walter S. Taylor (1931–2001)

The founder of the Taylor Wine Company had three sons and two daughters, all of whom worked in the winery, but in those days only sons took control when fathers retired. The sons produced only daughters with the sole exception of Walter Stephen Taylor, named after his grandfather and carrying on his shoulders alone the Taylor name to a third generation at New York's largest winery.

Walter was an independent-minded kid, privileged, a free spirit with a talent for drawing. His father, Greyton, sent him to military academy to groom him for the front lines of business. After college he "worked the floor" at the family winery learning each phase of operations during the years when Taylor became dominant in the industry. When, on Greyton's initiative, the company bought the Pleasant Valley winery, Walter became his father's assistant, running it as an independent Great Western Division.

Greyton Taylor was a close friend of Philip Wagner, traveled with him in Europe and brought back—by some accounts hidden in their suitcases—assorted varieties of the French hybrid grapevines dear to Wagner's heart. They became the core of Greyton and Walter's mission at Great Western to produce European-style New York table wines without input from California. In 1958, Walter bought back the original family winery on Bully Hill, idle since the business moved to Pleasant Valley at the outset of Prohibition. Most of the adjacent, nineteenth-century Taylor vineyards were gradually replanted with French hybrids.

Walter's reconnection with the Bully Hill homestead broadened his sense of family heritage into a fascination with the history of Finger Lakes viticulture and wine. He began collecting artifacts of the past hundred years from local barns, attics, junkyards, antique shops. One of the old winery buildings filled up with horse-drawn vineyard implements, hand pumps, cooper's tools, a copper pot-still, photographs of bygone wineries, diaries—a collection opened to the public in 1967 as the Finger Lakes Wine Museum. Modeled after museums in Europe, it was the first wine museum in America. Next to the museum Walter opened a shop selling home winemaking equipment, supplies, grape juice, and a book he illustrated and co-wrote with Great Western's winemaker Richard Vine: *Home Winemaker's Handbook.*

As the Taylor Wine Company changed during the 1960s from a family-run business into a publicly held corporation, the Great Western Division's independent status began to erode. Walter became increasingly disenchanted with company policy, above all with what he saw as its cautious adoption of French hybrids hand-in-hand with an increasing reliance on California blending wine. He believed passionately that hybrid varieties were the future of New York wine. With his father's backing Walter rehabilitated his grandfather's horse barn to resurrect the family winery on Bully Hill, initially calling it the Finger Lakes Wine Company. A trial-run vintage in 1969 amounted to 50 gallons. The following year the winery incorporated as Bully Hill Vineyards.

With his own operation now in place, though he was still executive vice-president of Taylor's Great Western Division, Walter went public with his criticism of winemaking practices at Taylor and other big New York wineries and indeed at the entire mainstream American wine industry. The occasion was a 1970 San Francisco convention of wine and spirits wholesalers. In an address to their luncheon gathering he lambasted winery executives (and alerted the media) for their use of chemicals and miscellaneous ingredients without public disclosure. The number of additives commonly used in wine cellars had multiplied in recent years. "If we don't start being absolutely honest with the public about what is in the bottle," he said, "we will be in a Ralph Nader situation."

Without naming individual brands he singled out his own state's wineries for selling New York-labeled wines that contained high percentages of California wine and water. To a degree this had been routine practice for nearly a century; but what started out as an aid for low-sugar, high-acid grapes had slipped since Prohibition into a profit-driven formula for mass-producing more out of less.

A month later the Taylor board of directors convened while company president Greyton was out of town. They voted to offer Walter a choice of retirement or dismissal; he chose to be fired. Bully Hill now became his citadel, where he could demonstrate "honest" winemaking and excoriate corporate profiteers.

Not inclined to immerse himself in cellar work, Walter hired a young German winemaker named Hermann Wiemer to ramp up Bully Hill's production. Wiemer's family had been in the wine business on the Mosel River for 300 years. His father ran Germany's largest grapevine nursery, responsible for replanting the Mosel's devastated vineyards after World War II. Trained at the famous Geisenheim wine institute, Wiemer had come to New York a couple of years earlier to work at the O-Neh-Da Winery on Hemlock Lake, hired through connections O-Neh-Da winemaker Leo Goering had at Geisenheim. Goering showed Wiemer around the vineyards and wineries of the Finger Lakes, when he met and went to work for Walter Taylor.

FIGURE 7.2. Walter S. Taylor with the Bully Hill mascot "Guilt-Free" in a Coke-littered example of his flair for publicity. As the sole grandson of the Taylor Wine Company's founder, he battled Coca-Cola for control of the family name in the late 1970s. (*Courtesy of Bully Hill Vineyards*)

The first commercial vintages at Bully Hill included varietals and blends made from French hybrid and native American grapes. The wines were often upstaged by their packaging. Walter regaled the bottles with his own often-whimsical artwork and elaborate back labels that saluted grower-suppliers and declared the cellar practices used, and not used. The phrases "Wine without Water" and "Wine without Guilt" figured prominently, along with Walter's signature and references to the Taylor family. His brochures included long lists of nefarious-sounding additives legally permitted but banned at Bully Hill.

To his delight, Walter displaced Konstantin Frank as the industry's number one thorn-in-the-side. Although Frank denigrated the French hybrids championed at Bully Hill, and Walter called Frank's beloved vinifera "wines to satisfy a few esoteric snobs," the two men got along surprisingly well, with much in common: obsessive, pugnacious personalities; disdain for the establishment; a flare for public relations; and a determination to remake Finger Lakes wine. Frank could not resist, though, with his Russian inflection, mispronouncing Walter's winery "Bull Hilly."

In 1972 Walter hung a huge painting in the wine museum that fanned a smoldering fire. It depicted a black train of California wine in tank cars crossing a trestle shored up by the contorted bodies of grape farmers. Along the tracks behind, gaunt figures of growers hung crucified on trellis posts. The religious allusion created an uproar in conservative Hammondsport. Rumors circulated that quirky Walter had lost his mind. Even many of his friends felt he had lost his bearings.

Stunned and shaken, Walter packed up and left town. He spent a year traveling around the country on what he called his "Johnny Grapeseed" tour, sometimes on his motorcycle, sometimes hitch-hiking, meeting with local media to spread the word about wine without guilt. The *Boston Herald American* wrote

> He's every inch a showman . . . [carrying] a backpack and bulging portfolio held together with string from which he produced, like a magician out of a hat, a seemingly endless assortment of objects including a sketch pad, oil paints, a couple of tennis rackets, a bunch of grapevines, and a few

bottles of his own wine . . . he also totes around a guitar slung across his back and a harmonica tucked in his pocket.

The winery regularly forwarded bottles for his impromptu tastings at venues of all description. Johnny Grapeseed's trademark bib-overalls disappeared for one of his favorite presentations at a nudist camp.

Walter returned to Bully Hill with batteries recharged; to some a genuine folk-hero, to some a buffoon. He relished both roles: "I decided to laugh at the whole thing, to laugh at life." Behind the laughter, though, the campaign against "wine factories" continued.

Mark Miller (1919–2008)

In the mid- to late-1800s the Hudson Valley was in its viticultural prime, a center for grape breeders and nurseries. One of the most prominent men spending their days dabbing pollen on grape flowers, Andrew Jackson Caywood, worked on a hillside above the village of Marlborough. Even when these hybridizers came up with a rare successful new variety, as Caywood did with the grape he named Dutchess, they almost always seemed to end their days sadly, with little recognition or financial reward.

So it went for A. J. Caywood. His vineyard declined with his fortunes and he died bitter and poor in 1889. Seventy years later a real estate agent brought Mark Miller up the dirt road to have a look at what was left, now owned by Caywood's grandson and nursed by an elderly black hired hand named Milton Barnes. It was at once a sad sight and a thrilling one, especially when Miller heard about its past.

Mark Miller was looking for vineyard land. He was a successful magazine illustrator working at a Manhattan studio, living in Westchester County, and infected with the strain of the wine bug that wants to set down roots. He had grown up in Oklahoma cotton country but fled to art school in Los Angeles, where he got a job as a sketch artist for costume design at 20th Century Fox Studios. Hobnobbing in Hollywood introduced him to wine.

After a stint in the army during World War II, he moved to New York City to pursue a career in magazine illustration. He was soon working with *Colliers*, the *Saturday Evening Post*, making good money and dabbling in home winemaking. That led to forays up the valley and to Marlboro. The motivation at this point was purely avocational: finding a country getaway to indulge his hobby.

He bought the Caywood property, about 40 acres, in 1957. It included narrowly terraced vineyards scaled to be worked with horses, descending in various stages of care, some feral, some still pruned and tilled by Milton Barnes and his horse. Most of the vines were Delawares, the variety held in highest esteem for winemaking in Caywood's time and used by him as parent material for much of his hybridizing. Delaware became the first wine Miller made from the property he named Benmarl.

Milton Barnes taught him the hands-on of grape growing; Everett Crosby's High Tor Vineyards, 40 miles south of Benmarl, served as a model; and Philip Wagner provided the textbook and the nursery to jumpstart Miller's dream. The following year, 1958, he planted test plots of 70 different varieties of wine grapes, mostly French hybrids but some vinifera and even a few Zinfandel vines from California—he was flush with the desire to research the Hudson Valley's vinicultural potential.

In a few years Miller was making enough wine to start thinking commercially, but not enough to afford New York's $1,500 winery license fee. He decided to wade into state politics, drafting a bill that would reduce fees and regulations and enable grape growers to start their own wineries. It was nipped in the legislative bud by lobbying from big Finger Lakes wine companies, notably Taylor. Why would they agree to encourage their suppliers to break away? Benmarl remained a hobby.

By the early 1960s the demand for magazine illustration began drying up as television and photojournalism took hold. Miller hired a caretaker for Benmarl and moved his young family to Europe, where the canvas artist was still in demand. He spent as much time as he could in Burgundy befriending and learning from some of its most celebrated vignerons; even proposing that Louis Latour take Benmarl under his wing. He didn't.

When he returned to America in 1967, recharged with Burgundian passion for winegrowing and with financial reserves from European commissions, Miller saw Benmarl in a transformative light: "The whim that had led me so blithely to buy the old vineyard as a pastime," he later wrote in his memoir, "had now become a vision of my farm as a kind of model for a cottage industry of small premium-quality wine producers . . . the apple-tree-filled valley had become in my mind the 'Cote d'Or' of America."

Like his friend Everett Crosby, Miller travelled in high society and could afford to venture into the shaky economics of Hudson Valley winegrowing, but unlike Crosby's personal adventure, Mark Miller's was a grand crusade. He professed "a moral obligation" to expose the practice of New York's wine establishment—blending sweet, grapey wines with a river of cheap, bulk California wine—"as aesthetically barren, financially greedy, and unfairly exploitative of the state's grape farmers, whose crops were rotting on the vine." It was the same message being trumpeted from Bully Hill, and Miller admired Taylor's bravura but he himself was too much the gentleman to join in combat. He resolved instead that Benmarl would rebel by example.

While in Europe Miller had sculpted a pair of elaborate bronze wine-cellar doorknobs. Now he set about building something to mount them on: a compact, Burgundy-flavored structure with vaults, spiral stairs, iron gates, and an art studio. The surrounding old vineyards were reshaped by bulldozer for tractor-wide terraces to accommodate Benmarl's first major plantings: French hybrid and vinifera. The dozen years of selling grapes and juice to home winemakers ended with a winery license in 1971. That first commercial vintage totaled 2,500 gallons. If Benmarl were to cover all the start-up costs for farm and winery equipment, license and bonding fees, vineyard expenses, bottles, corks, etc., and so on, added together, Miller figured the first-year cost per bottle was $750.

He now unveiled a marketing and development scheme of elegant design. For an annual fee, he offered subscribers what he called "vinerights:" the symbolic ownership of two grapevines. Each spring the vicarious grape growers of Benmarl's "Société des Vignerons" would gather at the winery to taste the new vintage and select a case for themselves, with their own personalized label. Membership became a social emblem. Minus the Burgundian trappings it was an idea widely adopted in later years as Community Supported Agriculture (CSA) and it was an immediate success. By 1975 Benmarl's hillside was fully planted and most of its wine flowed out through the Société.

One of the Société members was the new state commissioner of agriculture and markets, John Dyson. Another was the new governor, Hugh Carey, and *New York Times* wine columnist Frank Prial. The time had come to revive the old push for revision of New York's stifling, Prohibition-legacy regulation of winemaking. With his unique connections in Albany, Miller launched a campaign behind legislation that would drastically lower fees for farm-based producers and let them sell wine directly to consumers. This time there was little opposition.

Carey signed the farm winery bill into law in June 1976, a pivotal moment in the history of New York wine. In recognition of Mark Miller's leadership role, Benmarl, though it was already licensed, received New York Farm Winery License #1. Within days, membership in the Société des Vignerons doubled.

FIGURE 7.3. Mark Miller toward the end of his time as a winemaker, with vines dropping away toward the river. He had spearheaded passage of New York's Farm Winery Law, and his Benmarl Vineyards became the model for regeneration of Hudson Valley wine, but the dream of seeing a New-World Cote d'Or blanketing the surrounding slopes was still a wistful look in his eyes. (*Courtesy of Eric Miller*)

CHAPTER 8

Transformation

In Chautauqua and in Erie
All around the Finger Lakes
Snowsuits dot the hillsides
In between the vineyard stakes.
Those people brave the cold and wind
In their hoods and overshoes
And while they snip and trim their vines
They sing those Concord blues.

Well into the 1960s many vineyards throughout New York were still worked with horsepower. Nowhere was this more common than on the steep hillsides above Naples Valley. There a grower maneuvering his horse-pulled grape hoe might look down—seemingly across the span of a century—at the 3-million-gallon Widmer's wine complex on the valley floor, where winery president Ernest Reveal would be fretting "if within 10 years we may see the end of medium-sized wineries such as we are. They may not be able to sustain themselves in the crossfire of competition and the demand for capital."

New York's grape farmers were about to be bumped off their horses and taken for a wild, twentieth-century ride by an industry going through a wrenching transformation.

Reveal was looking over his shoulder at the Taylor Wine Company, an increasingly dominant presence in New York wine. Taylor's 10-million-gallon capacity had overflowed its old hillside collection of stone cellars, spilling into a campus of modern production plants on the flats of Pleasant Valley. Batteries of presses and tanks were fed by several hundred acres of company vineyards on Keuka Lake and several thousand acres under contract with growers throughout the Finger Lakes, the Chautauqua Grape Belt, and along Lake Ontario. Each year through the 1960s and into the 70s Taylor growers were encouraged to plant more vines and told which varieties to put in: native Americans (mostly Concord for sherry) and French hybrids, primarily Aurore, Baco Noir, and deChaunac. At the same time Nelson Shaulis's work at the Geneva Experiment Station was helping growers to boost their productivity from an average 1.5 tons per acre to 4 tons. The prices Taylor paid to growers set the standard for the region. It was, briefly, a heady time for New York winemakers and grape growers.

The winemaking regimen at Taylor, at least for its frontline generics, was typical of the major New York processors: blending old American varieties like Catawba, Concord, and Delaware with bulk wine from California and new inputs of French hybrids. Water and cane sugar were also routinely part of the mix. It was not uncommon for final blends to be up to one-third water and one-quarter Californian wine (the legal maximum for a New York label).

An exception was made for the production of sparkling wines, still done at Taylor in the traditional, labor-intensive, bottle-fermented *methode Champenoise*. Another exception was the Pleasant Valley Great Western brand. When it was acquired by Taylor in 1961, the Pleasant Valley Wine Co. continued to operate as an independent entity. In the course of the 1960s as the Taylor enterprise grew bigger and more complex, the three Taylor brothers began losing control to corporate managers. Greyton took refuge in the Great Western division, running it with his son Walter on their own agenda. In 1964 they introduced a line of wines made 100 percent from French hybrid grapes, the first in the Finger Lakes.

All of the growth at Taylor rested squarely on a national distribution network assembled by the company's brilliant marketing vice-president, Russell Douglas. Taylor became the only New York producer competing in the same retail arena with California majors Almaden and Paul Masson. Sales at Taylor increased annually by double-digits through the 60s.

In the Finger Lakes only two of Taylor's old rivals were still around: Widmer's Wine Cellars and Gold Seal Vineyards; the rest all

FIGURE 8.1. The Widmer's Wine Cellars complex in the 1960s. The white house near the left edge of the photo is the original homestead, with its vineyard behind. The hillside vineyards planted by Jacob Widmer and German immigrants were by now beginning to fade in favor of higher-yielding, easier-managed, valley-floor vineyards in the foreground. (*Courtesy of the Naples Library*)

casualties of Prohibition or its aftermath. At Widmer's, Ernest Reveal made the strategic decision to concentrate on white wine production in Naples and open a California branch for reds, flipping the industry practice of bringing tank-cars of California wine to New York, although Widmer's still did that too.

Like Taylor, Widmer's was planting both native American and French hybrid grape varieties in its 500 acres of company-owned vineyards, including those on the Naples flats. There, in the late-1960s, Widmer's introduced mechanical grape harvesters. The most dramatic feature of the Widmer winery was its enormous flat roof covered with barrels—twelve thousand barrels stacked four high—aging sherry in summer heat and winter snow for four years. The spectacle of Widmer's "rooftop cellar" added a public relations dividend to sound enological practice: the rigors of exposure to temperature extremes brought about chemical changes in the Concord–Niagara-based blend that had the effect of taming its wildly grapey flavors into a more mellow, nutty wine. From the rooftop it went underground for three more years of aging and vintage-blending in a traditional Spanish-style solera. The result: a very popular New York label in a fortified-wine market that, alas, was shrinking. U.S. sales of table wine overtook fortified dessert wine in 1968.

At Gold Seal Vineyards, Charles Fournier was president for most of the 1960s. Fournier was the renaissance man of New York wine. Given meager resources when he arrived in the Finger Lakes, he had created a Pink Catawba wine in the 1930s that resurrected Gold Seal (then called Urbana) from Prohibition purgatory. At the same time he began experimenting with French hybrids and, in his third decade at Gold Seal, he was working with Konstantin Frank on vinifera, taking New York wine down an exhilarating new path.

The commercial production of vinifera wines came while (perhaps because) Gold Seal owners Paul Schlem and Arthur Brody were running the business out of headquarters in New York City, letting Fournier manage affairs on Keuka Lake. By 1966 Gold Seal had 70 acres of vinifera vines in its vineyards; European-variety wine had tiptoed into mainstream New York production, albeit more-or-less through a back door—much of the wine went into blends with French hybrids for sparklers and still wines at-first labeled Chablis Natur and Rhine, a bow to marketing tradition and timidity.

During the 1960s a fourth major player in Finger Lakes wine came onto the field, a measure of the region's full recovery from the locust years. Canandaigua Industries had started in 1944 as a bulk supplier to bottlers, a branch of Little Joe Appelbaum's Long Island City-based Geffen Industries. Operating out of a former Canandaigua sauerkraut plant, and using the wooden sauerkraut fermentation vats, Appelbaum worked the same miracle that had proven so profitable in Queens, generating large quantities of bulk wine from small quantities of fruit.

Appelbaum sold the business in 1946 to his old employee Mack Sands, who installed his 22-year-old son Marvin to run it. After a rough

FIGURE 8.2. Clusters of botrytis-tinged vinifera grapes, a bottle of game-changing 1964 Gold Seal Riesling, and the man who remade Finger Lakes wine. Charles Fournier left Rheims, France, in 1934 on a one-year contract to help the Urbana Wine Company get on its feet after Prohibition. He stayed for half a century. (*Courtesy of the Glenn H. Curtiss Museum*)

start Marvin Sands began bottling under his own "Canandaigua" label and in 1953 he launched Richard's Wild Irish Rose, named after his son and a popular song. A 20-percent-alcohol blend from 70 percent local grapes and 30 percent California wine, it sold in rectangular, liquor-style bottles and became an instant hit on skid row. Dollar-per-ounce, it was the cheapest source of alcohol on the shelf. In 10 years annual sales of Wild Irish Rose hit $10 million, outpacing its major competition, Gallo Thunderbird.

Canandaigua now had the financial muscle to begin what would be its hallmark *modus operandi*: growth by acquisition. In 1965 Sands purchased the rights to Paul Garrett's "Virginia Dare" brand, giving Canandaigua a frayed but still-iconic national label. A few years later he bought the century-old Hammondsport Wine Company, adding sparkling wine to his portfolio. Company vineyards were not part of the plan; grapes could too easily be purchased cheaply on the open market from growers without contracts. Decisions at Canandaigua were guided by the control of costs. When Marvin Sands taught his son the art of winemaking, Richard Sands later recalled that a typical lesson examined strategies for maximizing the legally permitted dilution of wine with water.

In the Chautauqua Grape Belt, the Mogen David Wine Company took up residence at the central village of Westfield in 1967. The nation's largest producer of kosher Concord wine, Mogen David was based in Chicago and supplied by a network of vineyards that had radiated from Michigan to Ohio to Pennsylvania. Its need inevitably drew it to the heartland of the Concord grape, where the company bought 500 acres and three juice plants located provocatively close to the headquarters of Welch's Grape Juice Company. Mogen David quickly became the biggest processor of Chautauqua grapes after Welch, with a production capacity at Westfield of two million gallons.

Just one year after Mogen David moved into Westfield another winery came to town, a new venture of the Finger Lakes-based, fruit-juice-and-applesauce-maker Seneca Foods. Company president Arthur Wolcott had recently discovered the wines of Philip and Jocelyn Wagner's Boordy Vineyards. Impressed by their European style, he called the Wagners, flew his jet down to Baltimore and convinced them he could develop their Maryland experiment with French hybrid varieties into a national enterprise.

Starting with vintage 1968, the new Boordy made wine, at yet another defunct Westfield juice plant, from French hybrid grapes grown locally. The wines were marketed in accord with Phillip Wagner's desire to see American wines carry American regional names instead of bogus European labels like Burgundy. But there were not many French hybrid vineyards around Westfield in the 60s. In 1970 production moved to Garrett & Co.-era 1930s winery building in Penn Yan.

A transition was taking place, too, in the Hudson Valley. At crusty Brotherhood Wine Company, revival was underway after a long period of decline. Brotherhood had barely survived Prohibition and the years of Depression; the 1940s Schoonmaker-Marvel book *American Wines* described vineyards "long neglected and the plant is used mainly as a receiving depot for California bulk wines."

When new owners took over after the war, many of the cavernous cellars and vaults built during the winery's halcyon days were empty of wine, but they were still filled with history and the mystique of wine. Historian Leon Adams said Brotherhood's "ancient caves, which resemble those beneath old wineries in Europe, are the largest wine storage tunnels I have found in North America." They were also only 50 miles from New York City.

With the allure of its historic cellars Brotherhood virtually invented wine tourism in post-World War II New York. During the 1950s and 60s the company pulled out the last of John Jaques old vines to enlarge the winery parking lot. Cellar tours, concerts, and wine fests drew in crowds of 300,000 a year by the late 60s. Loyal customers were anointed into a Brotherhood of Wine Tasters, invited to special events. The wine selection favored sweet old crowd-pleasers like Catawba and Delaware, reviving Brotherhood's demand for local and western-New York grapes.

Farther up the valley in the village of Milton a cold storage warehouse became the new home of the Royal Kedem Wine Company. It had outgrown facilities in New York City run by Eugene Herzog, a sixth-generation winemaker. His orthodox Jewish family had started making wine in Austro-Hungary a century before Eugene emigrated to Manhattan's Lower East Side in 1948. In 20 years he had built up one of the state's major kosher wine companies.

The only Hudson region winery to soldier through Prohibition and the years after, reasonably intact, was the Bolognesi family's Hudson Valley Wine Company, carried along in an insular way by its own 350-acre vineyard, close-knit family control, and close ties with area monasteries. The Bolognesis had settled into their self-contained, Old-World-style wine estate with no grander ambitions than to pay the bills, nurture the family and make good wine—a quiet, gentle model that began to fray with the passing of generations, dimming memories of Italy, and a new business order. The Monsieur Henri wine importing firm bought the family estate from aging heirs in 1967 (briefly hiring

Mark Miller as director). Two years later Monsieur Henri itself became a subsidiary of PepsiCo. The monastically inclined Bolognesi estate had drifted into the realm of high-powered beverage acquisitions.

In the Finger Lakes, Widmer's Wine Cellars was also changing hands, purchased from its Rochester owners by the R. T. French (mustard) Company, which was in turn a division of the British food and wine conglomerate Reckitt & Coleman—the first case of foreign ownership in New York wine and a sign of the perceived strength of the industry.

There were many signs of strength. Sales at most of the big wineries grew steadily into the 1970s. Vineyard acreage was also growing again in the Finger Lakes and western New York after decades of stagnation. The planting of French hybrid varieties seemed to signal a new era; there were 2,500 bearing acres by 1974, beginning to have an impact on the composition and character of New York wines. They were showing some signs of drying out, lightening up, becoming less assertively grapey as the use of Concord receded, even to some degree in kosher and dessert wines.

Taylor was now, in the early 1970s, the largest wine producer outside California and the largest sparkling winemaker in the nation. In the spring of 1975, 375 acres were added to its existing 875 acres of company vineyards and they still accounted for only 10 percent of the grapes trucked to Hammondsport. Most of these new vineyards were going in along both shores of Seneca Lake, where Gold Seal too was buying up farms.

In February of 1975 a journalist-turned-grape-grower-turned-journalist again, William Moffett, with his partner Hope Merletti, published the first issue of New York's first periodical for grape growers since the turn of the century. *Eastern Grape Grower* magazine was another sign of renaissance, like its nineteenth-century analogs, disseminating the latest viticultural practices, technologies, and research on new varieties. It soon added "*& Winery News*" to the title, reporting on the evolving wine scene as a business and technical journal. The magazine sponsored workshops and a conference—Wineries Unlimited—recording and fostering the resurgence of regional wineries.

Embedded in all of these developments, however, was trouble ahead. Big increases in vineyard acreage had an ominous history of overproduction and collapsing markets dating back to the 1850s. While they were planting and contracting more vineyards, the big processors were also steadily increasing their use of California bulk wine. When R. T. French took over Widmer's they established a 500-acre vineyard in Sonoma County's Alexander Valley, not a vote of confidence in New York farms.

Corporate managers with national marketing goals logically pursued a kind of transcontinental wine formula that attempted to homogenize East and West. An "American" appellation appeared on labels, flaunting the European tradition of varietal specialization within regional identities. At first it seemed to work. Sales increased, but the numbers masked a gloomier trend: New York's share of the resurgent American table wine market had been 16 percent in 1966. Nine years later it dropped to 10 percent and continued to fall—a shrinking slice of a growing pie. It went the other way with dessert wines. California wineries were gradually shifting their production from fortified to table wines, ceding more of the dessert market to New York—a bigger slice of a shrinking pie.

Sales at Taylor and other major producers flattened out by the mid-70s just as recent vineyard plantings came into bearing, yields increased, and the state's grape crop swelled. The wineries began switching long-term contracts with growers to annual renewals. The *Syracuse Herald-Journal* warned "farmers are at the mercy of the wineries when new contracts are negotiated at the end of the harvest for the next year." Late in 1975, sitting on swollen inventories, Taylor amended all contracts with growers to let the company buy only part of their crop. Other wineries followed. The following fall, for the first time since Prohibition, grapes were left to rot on the vines.

The mavericks profiled in Chapter 7 had begun breaking away from mainstream New York wine production in the 1960s when it was still growing stronger, but the industry started genuinely breaking apart in 1976, the year the grape market soured and the year New York finally passed a farm winery law.

Attempts to loosen the state's restrictive, Prohibition-era wine laws had circulated in Albany for more than a decade, routinely undermined by stakeholders in the status quo: major producers, wholesalers, retailers, even complacent growers. The prospects for reform changed when the election of Governor Hugh Carey coincided with turmoil in the grape market. Carey was a wine drinker, a member of Benmarl

Vineyard's Société des Vignerons and, as such, a party to Mark Miller's vision of a state blooming with artisanal wine estates.

The governor gave Lieutenant Governor Mary Anne Krupsak, another wine-and-food maven, the job of getting a farm winery law through the legislature. Krupsak laid the groundwork by barnstorming the state in a series of meetings with processors and growers, listening dutifully, then informing them that the Carey administration was going to make this happen. Wine companies, on the eve of gutting grape contracts, had little to say. Objections from retailers fell on deaf ears. Historically passive growers found themselves being mobilized by their lieutenant governor.

The "Farm Wineries and Cider Mills Low-Cost License Law" sailed through the legislature, taking effect with Carey's signature in June 1976. It created a new license category—annual fee $125—for growers making less than 50,000 gallons of wine from their own fruit. Even more importantly, it lifted restrictions on selling wine at retail; farm wineries were free to bypass wholesalers and sell all their production direct to consumers, restaurants and stores within New York State.

Glenora Wine Cellars and Heron Hill Vineyards in the Finger Lakes and the Merritt Estate in Chautauqua were first to take advantage of the new law; opening in 1977. They were emblematic of two very different kinds of entrepreneurs about to revive New York's small-scale, farm-based winemaking in the coming decades.

On Seneca Lake a group of growers led by long-time fruit farmer Eastman Beers had enlisted early-on in Krupsak's campaign. With vineyards on both sides of the lake losing crop allocations to Taylor, they had plans in place, before the governor's signature, to build Seneca's first winery since Prohibition in Beers' vineyard above Glenora Point. Most of their varieties were French hybrids but Glenora Wine Cellars' debut 1977 vintage included a first crop from vinifera plantings. It was made by a new graduate of the University of California's school of enology at Davis, John Williams.

Heron Hill Vineyards was the brainchild of Peter Johnstone, a refugee copywriter from Madison Avenue ad firms. When he read in 1967 about Konstantin Frank's success growing vinifera on Keuka Lake, Johnstone drove upstate to scout Frank's neighborhood, found a grape farm for sale with a dazzling view of the lake, and bid farewell to city life. He had never sat on a tractor. He spent the next 10 years learning how to farm as he gradually ripped out native American grapevines and replanted with Riesling and Chardonnay. He also drew up plans for a winery nestled into the shoulder of Bully Hill, and waited for an investor. A Rochester native named John Ingle, another back-to-the-lander with his own vineyard on Canandaigua Lake, came along when the Farm Winery Law opened the door.

In the Chautauqua County town of Forestville, Bill Merritt was one of the few local grape growers who latched onto Krupsak's barnstorming farm-winery campaign. His fruit farm had been in the family since vineyards spread along Lake Erie in the 1880s. Hit hard by the shriveling market for grapes, he signed on for the Grape Belt's first new small-winery license.

The law was designed to throw a lifeline to grape farms losing their markets, and it did that for the Merritts and the Woodbury family in Chautauqua, for Beers, the Wagners, Hunts, Fulkersons and Stamps (Lakewood Vineyards) in the Finger Lakes—some of them were family farms dating back to military land grants from the Revolutionary War.

But more often, as it turned out, the lifeline drew in people with no connection to farming whatsoever, just a love of wine, a restlessness in their careers, perhaps visions of arcadia. As Johnstone put it, "The line between work and pleasure blurs. It seems like somebody tapped me on the shoulder and said 'You don't have to work this lifetime.'" (In the end it would still be work.) The first neophyte winegrowers came from all professional directions: Kodak executive Robert McGregor (McGregor Vineyard Winery), book editor Walter Pederson (Four Chimneys Farm Winery), Cornell University educators Robert and Mary Plane (Cayuga Vineyards), New York City tugboat pilot Bill Lucas and his wife Ruth (Lucas Vineyards), novelist William Wetmore (Cascade Mountain Vineyards), graphic artist Ben Feder (Clinton Vineyards), neurosurgeon George Green (North East Vineyards), IBM executive Lou Fiore (West Park Vineyards), home-builder Andrew Colaruotolo (Casa Larga Vineyards), foodies Alexander and Louisa Hargrave (Hargrave Vineyards), restaurateurs Peter and Patricia Lenz (Lenz Winery), air traffic controller Ray Blum (Peconic Bay Vineyards), fuel-oil-company owner Kip Bedell (Bedell Cellars).

In 1978, while he was visiting family in Germany for Christmas, Bully Hill winemaker Hermann Wiemer received a telegram from Walter Taylor: he was fired. It was not unexpected, nor unprepared for. Wiemer had purchased a soybean farm on Seneca Lake and spent the past six years planting his own vineyard, exclusively with vinifera varieties, mostly Riesling. Hermann J. Wiemer Vineyards winery opened the same year he left Bully Hill, with Taylor's telegram framed on the tasting room wall. His label featured a family crest recalling a 300-year tradition of winemaking on the Mosel River.

The business of vineyards and wine did not lend itself to hurried start-ups; there was no rush of farm wineries under the new law. New licenses averaged a few each year. Still that was a sea change in an industry that had seen only a few new labels for decades. It echoed the appearance of wineries a century earlier, when grape farmers were also reacting to an imbalance of supply and demand.

Alongside the unfolding of small wineries came the introduction of a new generation of wine-grape varieties hybridized from European and American species. The long history of interspecific hybrids began with chance crossings of grapevines imported from Europe with wild native vines in the early 1800s, continued through the painstaking work of independent breeders like A. J. Caywood and Jacob Moore in the late 1800s, and the breeding program at the Geneva Experiment Station under U. P. Hedrick after the turn of the twentieth century. Developing new varieties of many different fruits and vegetables was a core part of the station's original mandate, and new varieties for the table-grape market appeared regularly, but none specifically for wine.

That changed after 1962 when the state's prohibition-era funding restrictions were officially lifted. Within several years the breeding program released a variety named Cayuga White. Widmer's Wine Cellars made the first varietal Cayuga White in 1976, a testament to Widmer's fading tradition of innovation with varietals. The new variety found its true home in a new crop of small wineries more agile and more focused on regional specialties. Farm wineries would be the seedbed for more new varieties to come out of Geneva and elsewhere.

The emergence of farm wineries would change the face of New York wine but it would be a mistake to overstate their immediate impact. Five years after the Farm Winery Law took effect, small wineries accounted for barely 2.5 percent of the state's wine output. New York wine was still solidly dominated by the major processors—Taylor,

Gold Seal, Widmer's, Canandaigua, Monarch, Mogen David—and the high-stakes process of corporate acquisition was escalating.

In January 1977 the Coca-Cola Company of Atlanta, with $3 billion of sales worldwide, purchased the $60-million-sales Taylor Wine Company. The reaction in New York's wine community mixed optimism—that Coke's resources and marketing muscle could revive Taylor sales and production—with wariness of distant, mega-overlords. The Taylor Company's most vocal critic, Walter Taylor, told the *Rochester Democrat & Chronicle*, "I think it's going to be one of the best things that could happen to Hammondsport. Coca-Cola is one of the best-managed companies in the United States." They were fateful words. Under Coke ownership, one of the Taylor Company's first moves was a lawsuit filed against Bully Hill Vineyards for trademark infringement, blocking the use of Walter Taylor's name on his labels.

The Taylor name had become increasingly prominent on recent vintages of Bully Hill labels and Coke had a history of fierce trademark protection. Walter also had a history of defending the family name, as its only male heir, and he relished a fight. He threw himself into a campaign of public relations stunts, beginning with a battalion of sympathetic students from nearby Cornell University bussed to the winery for a "No-Name Party," blacking out the Taylor name on his inventory of brochures and bottles. He organized a parade of goats up Bully Hill behind a banner declaring "They've taken my name but they won't get my goat." The goat became the symbol of Walter's struggle against corporate power. A sketch of his pet goat "Guilt Free" appeared on Bully Hill labels. Walter dragged a railroad tank-car up Bully Hill to trumpet Taylor's increasing use of California bulk wine. The media loved it; a feature-writer's dream, with plenty of photo-ops. News stories amplified Walter's tirades against the company's winemaking practices: one of his favorite quips—"You can always tell Taylor is making wine when the level of Keuka Lake drops."

A series of court appeals and injunctions ultimately left Bully Hill on the losing end of its legal struggle with Taylor Wine. But during the nearly three years of their David-and-Goliath drama the sales of Bully Hill wines quadrupled. Walter had lost the trademark battle and won the public relations war.

Barely a year after Coca-Cola took control of Taylor the company announced the creation of Taylor California Cellars, a line of California wines with a 3-million-gallon initial run, much of it to be bottled in Hammondsport for eastern distribution. Contracts with Taylor growers continued to be trimmed or dropped as tank-cars rolled into the Finger Lakes. A new-release Taylor American Chablis consisted of 80 percent California French Colombard, 20 percent New York Aurore. It became clear that Coca-Cola valued Taylor for its national brand recognition and distribution network, two keys to Coke's own success with soda. The Taylor Wine Company was now part of a group of Coke's subsidiary wineries, East and West, called The Wine Spectrum, based in California. Taylor's own director of grower relations later lamented that his company was "under the wing of an organization very prejudiced against our products."

At the same time, Coca-Cola acted to shore up its New York venture. It constructed a huge new barrel-aging facility to accommodate swollen inventories and it expanded the effort at Taylor's Great Western division to create a high-end line of vintage-dated, regional-appellation wines from French-American hybrids.

Coca-Cola had outbid a number of other parties interested in Taylor, among them the Canadian-based liquor conglomerate Seagram Company. Joseph E. Seagram's bootlegging operation during Prohibition had grown into an international spirits empire, lately expanding to include wine as Americans' drinking habits evolved—in 1980 Americans drank more wine than distilled spirits for the first time in the nation's history. Two years after Coke bought Taylor, Seagram bought Taylor's Keuka Lake neighbor Gold Seal Vineyards.

The experience of Gold Seal under Seagram paralleled that of Taylor under Coke. Having recently acquired the much larger Paul Masson wine firm, Seagram was heavily invested in California. When sales at Gold Seal failed to keep pace with production, grower contracts and grape prices were cut. The company's pioneering work with vinifera shriveled to a sideline eventually dismissed as uneconomical, the logical conclusion of an enterprise making European-variety wines much more cheaply in California. Charles Fournier, retained as a figurehead honorary president until his death in 1983, ended his long career publicly lauded, privately disconsolate.

It took the Coca-Cola Company just six years to determine they were not accomplishing with wine what they had done with soda. In the fall of 1983 they announced the sale of their Wine Spectrum subsidiaries, including Taylor, to the Seagram Company for $200 million dollars. Coke's wine venture had failed but in the end still managed to return a profit.

Seagram had now swallowed up major competitors in New York and California. Consolidation was the order of the day and people around Keuka Lake sensed what would come next. Seagram consolidated all its winemaking operations at Taylor's modern campus south of Hammondsport and closed down the 120-year-old Gold Seal chateau, the jewel of nineteenth-century New York wineries. In the 1980s, isolated by a lake no longer useful for shipping and by steep hills barring any access by rail, the old cellars were obsolete.

After two decades running Widmer's Wine Cellars, the R. T. French Company also exited Finger Lakes wine in 1983, through a management-employee buyout. Widmer's president Charles Hetterich led a valiant effort to remake the old winery around traditional benchmarks of local ownership and regional wine identity. Either too late or premature, it was not to be. In three years Widmer's fell into the portfolio of the Canandaigua Wine Company.

Through all the turmoil in New York wine and grape markets, Canandaigua consistently prospered. In the early 1980s annual production at the old sauerkraut plant approached 20-million gallons, nearly two-thirds of it Richard's Wild Irish Rose. Year after year the company's financial report posted record profits, reflecting not just the soaring sales touted in press releases but also "a material decrease in product costs," specifically the declining cost of California bulk wine and plummeting market prices for New York grapes. In 1985, when Seagram–Taylor–Gold Seal cancelled all grower contracts and bought everything on the open market, grape prices slid to an average $182 per ton, below most growers' cost of production. Through a dummy agent, Canandaigua offered $75 a ton for uncontracted Concords.

Canandaigua's healthy cash flow enabled the company to buy the iconic Widmer's Wine Cellars and, in the same year, purchase the Manischewitz brand from Monarch Wine Company. Widmer's underutilized facilities in Naples became the new home of Manischewitz's 1.5-million-case output: Canandiagua's portal into the kosher wine market.

"The Concord Blues"

A song written and sung by Douglas Knapp, president of the NY State Wine Grape Growers, at the 1984 NY Wine Council Annual Dinner.

In Chautauqua and in Erie
All around the Finger Lakes
Snowsuits dot the hillsides
In between the vineyard stakes.
Those people brave the cold and wind
In their hoods and overshoes
And while they snip and trim their vines
They sing those Concord blues.

Oh, should we pull those blues out?
And plant 'em back to what?
Should we be planting peaches,
or maybe coconuts?
Oh Lord, give us direction
Oh, tell us what to do.
Meanwhile join us in a verse
Or two of Concord blues.

Before old Prohibition
Their industry was tall
But since Repeal in '33
They've had little growth at all.
They want to grow 'em, squeeze 'em
And put 'em in a keg
But laws have got 'em hamstrung
Stomping grapes on just one leg.

Albany's going to help us
They're puttin' on a drive.
Only wine in food stores
Will keep us alive.
Don't want no jams & jellies bills

A pittance just won't do.
We've got to have more markets
To forget those Concord blues.

Now gather round you growers
I'll tell you what we'll do,
We'll juice those grapes, ferment 'em up
And make a keg or two.
Then when we're on welfare
And winter nights are cold
We'll pull out the bottle
And drink those Concord blues.

While the Farm Winery Law helped a handful of grape farms become wine estates, most farmers didn't have the resources, the skills, or even the interest to jump into a business fraught with challenges. The creation of an alternative, small-winery market for grapes was a long-term proposition; the crisis for farmers was immediate. Many were unable to make payments on loans taken out in the 1960s and 70s to plant more vines at the behest of wineries. Statewide, hundreds of acres of vineyard were being abandoned or ripped out each year: 9,000 acres lost in a dozen years.

One response to the crisis proposed a grape marketing order, raising money for the promotion of New York wine through a small assessment on each gallon of wine sold by the state's wineries. A similar plan had worked in California but it depended on industry-wide cooperation. Taylor refused to go along. Why would they pay to promote New York when most of their wine was made in California?

Another proposal, pushed by Governor Mario Cuomo and the New York State Wine Grape Growers Association, called for the sale of New York wines in grocery stores. For the 50 years since Prohibition bills had regularly been put forward in the state legislature to permit the sale of wine in food stores and for 50 years they had been scuttled by the opposition of wholesalers and retailers guarding their turf. This time only New York wines were included, and though they accounted for just 7 percent of wine sales in liquor stores, lobbyists once more blocked the bill in legislative committee.

A third proposal did succeed: creation of a New York Wine & Grape Foundation, an organization to support research and promotion for all the state's grape products, initially entirely state-funded but programmed to gradually phase onto industry support. A small staff set up shop in Penn Yan with a two-million-dollar budget. The foundation would mature and grow hand-in-hand with the state's small winery sector: a long, slow process.

Mainstream New York wine limped through the 80s with the aid of wine coolers, a faddish mix of wine, fruit juice, and carbonation, allowed on grocery shelves as low-alcohol cousins of beer. They propped up the native-variety market for a dwindling number of grape farms, until the cooler fad began to fizzle by 1990.

Ultimately there was no quick fix for the faltering Old Order, dinosaur wineries disconnected from their vineyard roots. The transition to a new paradigm had to run its wrenching course. Abandoned, overgrown vineyards were a familiar sight along New York lakes, studded with tilting trellis posts like the stones of old cemeteries. The decline of the state's total vineyard acreage bottomed out in the early 1990s, just as the emergence of small, farm wineries gained momentum.

As their numbers increased, new wineries tended to align with one or the other of the two most prominent revolutionaries of the 60s: Bully Hill Vineyards and Vinifera Wine Cellars. Most of the newcomers created wine lists mixing the French hybrids championed by Walter Taylor with old native varieties like Catawba, new Geneva hybrids like Cayuga White, and some viniferas, offering a wine for every taste. They included Glenora, Merritt Estate, Wagner, Cascade Mountain, Woodbury, Hazllitt, Swedish Hill, Hunt Country, Four Chimneys, Fulkerson, Lakewood.

Another group followed the Euro-centric doctrine of Konstantin Frank. It had nothing to do with his rants against hybrids; they had expired with the old man. Son Willy Frank and grandson Fred carried on at Vinifera Wine Cellars with the simple conviction that the classic European varieties made the best wine. They pared down the 30-odd varieties in Dr. Frank's experimental vineyard to a handful of aromatic, cool-climate whites plus a few promising reds, making primarily dry wines targeted to a cosmopolitan market.

Hermann Wiemer became Frank's highest-profile apostle in the Finger Lakes, honing the focus more directly onto Riesling. Among the other vinifera-based farm wineries: Lamoreaux Landing, Millbrook, Anthony Road, McGregor, Red Newt, Silver Thread, Ravines, Shalestone, Standing Stone, along with Hargrave, Lenz, and all the other wineries springing up on Long Island (that story belongs to the next chapter.)

Vinifera Wine Cellars and Bully Hill served not just as models but as mentors, rubber-boot-camps for apprentice winemakers moving on to run the new generation of cellars. Veterans of Bully Hill went on to Hermann Wiemer Vineyards, Glenora, Lucas, Chateau Lafayette Reneau, Wagner, and Poplar Ridge Vineyards. Vinifera Wine Cellars was the training ground for winemakers at Lenz, Fox Run, and Ravines.

Against the backdrop of small wineries recolonizing the state's old vineyard districts, the end-game of New York's nineteenth-century wine establishment played out. Under Seagram ownership the Taylor–Gold Seal operation continued to deteriorate until company executives, led by Gold Seal veteran Paul Schlem, arranged a bank-financed management buy-out of the entire Seagram wine division, calling themselves Vintners International. With a heavy debt load and primary interest, once again, in California subsidiaries, Vintners proceeded to cash out what was left of value in Hammondsport. The campus of more than 50 buildings, stripped of winemaking equipment, was eventually sold off to the Mercury Aircraft Corporation.

In 1993 Canandaigua Wine Company bought all remaining assets of Vintners International for less than $150 million. Canandaigua now owned all the famous old names of Finger Lakes wine—Taylor, Great Western, Gold Seal, Widmer—but "the assets that we most coveted," CEO Richard Sands explained in his book, *Reaching for the Stars*, "were Taylor California Cellars and Paul Masson . . . Essentially we are able to eliminate their [Vintner International's] entire organization and basically subsume the sales and marketing, as well as the management of their production organization, under our umbrella . . . In fact, we planned on some of those brands continuing to decline."

The acquisition of Vintners made Canandaigua the second largest wine producer in the United States, after E. & J. Gallo. New York brands represented a tiny fraction of its holdings; the name Canandaigua had to go. In 2000 the firm became Constellation Brands; its stated mission: "to double in size every five years." Coincidentally, that was close to the rate at which farm wineries were opening across the state. The growth of New York's wine industry had achieved a bizarre kind of symmetry.

There was now one mega-wine company, a couple of large producers of kosher wines, and a rising tide of almost 300 small-to-very-small farm-based wineries. With production levels typically well below 10,000 gallons a year, the new generation of wineries quickly found their marketing niche in direct sales to visitors. Brotherhood and Bully Hill had demonstrated some of the methods and the huge potential of wine tourism. In 1983 a half-dozen wineries on Cayuga Lake determined that they were individually too small to draw many visitors but collectively they could be a stronger destination. They formed the state's and the nation's first wine trail.

In time there were almost 20 wine trails on three other Finger Lakes, along the Lake Erie and Niagara escarpments, in the North Country, on Long Island, and on both sides of the Hudson River. They were wildly successful at bringing people to wineries and selling wine. Some began to stage regular, ticketed events that drew larger crowds, inevitably sometimes looking more for a merry outing than a wine for dinner. Wineries increasingly found themselves in the entertainment business with staffs of tour guides, event planners, tasting room servers, even parking attendants. The profile of sales at trail events nudged production (especially upstate) toward sweet-and-fruity party wines.

The Finger Lakes wine region, in particular, was facing an identity crisis. It was successfully exploiting the legacy of native American varieties even as it attempted to erase that image with European-style, food-oriented wines, notably Riesling. The district's northern-latitude cool climate, its shale-laced soils and long German-immigrant history all favored the culture of Riesling. The variety survived hard winters and produced reliable quantities of fine wine even in the toughest growing season. By the turn of the twenty-first century, as winemakers in the Old and New Worlds became more adept at crafting drier styles, Riesling gained stature as one of the world's greatest wines—and the Finger Lakes arguably made America's best.

At the same time wines with names like Foxy Lady, Sweet Rosie, and Red Cat flew off winery shelves. The grapes were cheap, plentiful, and easy to grow; the wines were cash cows. The penultimate example was Hazlitt Vineyard's Red Cat, a wine made from the same Catawba grape that gave birth to Finger Lakes viticulture in early nineteenth-century Hammondsport. It became such a spectacular seller for the Seneca Lake winery they leased unused production facilities at the huge Taylor plant in Hammondsport, then moved again to take over Widmer's Wine Cellars in Naples. Hazlitt purchased that production complex from Constellation Brands in 2011 and renamed it Red Cat Cellars. In that year Red Cat, with its cartoon label, outsold all the vinifera wines made in the Finger Lakes.

The New York Wine & Grape Foundation—the official voice of all the state's wineries—had grown by now, under its energetic president, Jim Trezise, into an organization with a political acuity honed as much by intra-industry dynamics as by Albany lobbying. It had the daunting job of advocating for everyone from Constellation Brands and Welch Foods to the dreamiest back-road micro-winery, and projecting some sort of cohesive image. The result, inevitably, was promotion for the extraordinary diversity of the state's wine—from old American grapes, European varieties, French hybrids, Geneva hybrids, it was truly the most eclectic collection of any wine region in the world. Some winemakers grumbled that the Foundation's message only perpetuated image problems from the past.

On Long Island, the state's newest community of winegrowers discretely distanced itself from the messy, compromised narrative tied to New York's upstate legacy.

CHAPTER 9

Long Island

For the first ten years-plus quite honestly no one had a clue of how to go about it and do it properly.

The business of winegrowing on Long Island did not start well. It began with the first English governor of the New York colony, Richard Nicolls, described by the dean of Island historians Benjamin Thompson as "uniting in himself all the attributes of despotic authority." In 1665 the flagrantly corrupt Nicolls granted a friend in Brooklyn not only the exclusive right to grow and sell wine without being taxed, but the legal authority to demand five shillings per acre, annually for 30 years, from anyone else who might entertain planting vines on Long Island.

There is no record whether Nicoll's crony ever actually made wine or even planted vines, but the scheme would effectively squelch other early attempts to grow Long Island wine.

Not until a century-and-a-half later did the Prince family and later Andre Parmentier and Alphonse Loubat do heroic work with wine grapes in Brooklyn and Queens. Their stories, told in an earlier chapter, belong more to developments in the Hudson Valley than to Long Island. On the island's East End, a Frenchman named Moses Fournier reportedly grew grapes at Cutchogue in the early eighteenth century, by some accounts with help from local Indians. There are records of other Fournier vineyards in Southold and in Southampton.

In his 1846 book, *The Cultivation of American Grape Vines and Making of Wine*, Alden Spooner wrote "in the early settlement of Long Island a vineyard was cultivated near Southampton, by Mr. Fournier. We understand very good wild Grapes [feral hybrids?] are now in great plenty in the woods and swamps near that place . . . and have been successfully used for wine."

Long Island's first commercial winery had a brief run on the western shore of Stony Brook Harbor at Nissiquogue, in the 1880s. There Thomas Seabury had established an extensive collection of wine grape varieties on his estate Rassapeage. When John Ruszits bought the property he added a wine cellar next to the vineyard and started marketing the first Long Island wine, earning a local following for his Rassapeage Claret. But the business apparently produced no more than a few vintages.

Fruit-growing was often a part of Long Island farms, but rarely their focus. On the East End, potatoes started pushing out other crops late in the nineteenth century, favored by light, acidic soil and advanced by the invention in Southold of a mechanical digger. Polish and Irish immigrant farmers moved into the area. Potato fields spread across the island until, at their peak in 1952, they covered more than 60,000 acres, pocked with half-buried storage barns. Enter the Colorado potato beetle, the inevitable uninvited guest of such monoculture.

Cornell University ran a research station at Riverhead that began encouraging farmers to consider alternative crops. A spotlight fell on the Cutchogue farm of the Wickham family, an island of diversity in the sea of spuds. John Wickham grew scores of vegetables and fruits on what he called the old Indian broadfields, land worked by his family for 250 years and by the Corchaug people for centuries before. The first European settlers found an Indian village surrounded by some 240 acres under cultivation, thought to be the largest single field of crops in pre-Columbian America. Around 1960 Wickham contacted Cornell, his alma mater, seeking advice about adding grapes to the peaches, pears, cherries, and cranberries offered at the Wickham roadside farm stand, a North Fork landmark. The pomologists at Cornell's Geneva Experiment Station replied that they had no experience with grapes on the island, would he be interested in working together on field trials?

The Wickham farm became a de facto Cornell research branch, growing dozens of grape varieties including many European vinifera, some of them Mediterranean cultivars putting New York State's warmest climate to the test. John Wickham also worked with Konstantin Frank. At a Cornell seminar in January 1962 Frank declared "I see no reason why we shall not or cannot grow delicious table varieties—Perlette, Delight, Beauty and some others—on the sands of Long Island. Here a new industry can be started for many farmers of this area to supply New York City as well as New York State and vicinity with fresh, delicious table grapes of high quality."

Wickham did not drink wine. He bought vines from Frank but only table varieties for the farm stand. Muscat Ottonel was one of Frank's favorite grapes, an exotic that performed well in the Cutchogue vineyard but, as it turned out, not so well at the farm stand. Customers found the flavor too strange and they objected to seeds. When Wickham pulled out his muscat vines, Frank was characteristically incensed: "Three thousand years to develop that grape and now you want it be seedless!"

The trunks of John Wickham's 10-year-old, ungrafted vinifera grapevines were as thick as his forearm when a young couple paid a visit on the day before Thanksgiving 1972. Alexander and Louisa Hargrave had spent their first year out of graduate school at Harvard surveying the East and West Coasts for a place to grow vinifera grapes for wine, Cabernet Sauvignon above all. Like Goldilocks, they found some options too hot (Napa Valley, Virginia), some too cold (the Finger Lakes, Massachusetts). When they asked Cornell pomologist John Tomkins for advice, he first vainly proposed they plant French hybrids, then told them to go see John Wickham.

Wickham also discouraged them. They were starry-eyed suburbanite wine lovers with almost no training and no experience, never having grown even a backyard garden or made a carboy of wine. But Wickham's little vineyard whispered seductively over his shoulder, confirming that everything the Hargraves had read about the East End climate sounded just right. Within a few months they were owners of a 66-acre potato farm with storage barn and a weary, seventeenth-century house, not far from the Wickhams. Barely two months after that, in May 1973, they planted 17 acres of Cabernet Sauvignon, Pinot Noir, and Sauvignon Blanc.

This was virgin territory for a commercial wine vineyard. Someone was going to have to stumble onto the bottom of the learning curve and the Hargraves wasted no time. They rushed to plant an under-prepared field, then battled weeds and problems with soil composition for years. Their first-year vines were grafted by Hermann Wiemer at Bully Hill Vineyards on a vigorous rootstock that, in potato ground heavily fertilized for decades, produced rank, bushy growth—exacerbating mildew and mold problems. A horde of rabbits chewed back the tender new shoots of Sauvignon Blanc.

The Hargraves's second-year vines arrived from a California nursery infected, it turned out, with virus. Most of these early vines had short lives. In year three Hurricane Belle defoliated the newest vines. Hargrave Vineyard's first vintage, from the 1975 harvest released in 1977, consisted primarily of a light Cabernet aged too long in American oak barrels made for whiskey: an orange-tinged wine desperately labeled as nonvintage rosé. Louisa later said "We made so little of this wine that we had a 'no tasting' policy. We said we couldn't give away something so precious, but in reality, we would have sold considerably less wine if people had been able to taste it first." Early vintages were also dogged by unevenness from the practice of bottling one barrel at a time.

Lifestyle writers lauded the Hargraves for leading the way of East End agriculture from potatoes to wine. Professional wine critics generally held their fire. Despite all its woes, the phenomenon of Hargrave Vineyards swung the door open to Long Island viniculture. Many of the winemakers who followed credited Alex and Louisa as their inspiration; some apprenticed in the vineyard or as cellar rats. The wines improved dramatically as the learning curve lifted and when Michigan winemaker Dan Kleck came on board in 1979. The 1980 Hargrave Merlot opened many eyes to the potential of a new American wine district.

The Hargraves's arrival created a stir in the NOFO neighborhood; they were considered a couple of hippie interlopers, but they were a magnet for people open to change. Christian and Rosamond Baiz bought vines from the Hargraves in their second spring, to plant a half-acre experiment on a Southhold potato farm that had been in the Baiz family for six generations. It was the germ of Old Field Vineyards Winery.

FIGURE 9.1. Louisa and Alex Hargrave during their initiation as Long Island winegrowers. The hoe was her constant companion as weeds besieged the young vineyard. His hand was badly injured by a shattered carboy as he experimented in making wine. (*Courtesy of the Cutchogue New Suffolk Free Library*)

An airline pilot with an unpromising name for a would-be grape grower, David Mudd, ran into the Hargraves at an equipment auction during their first summer in Cutchogue. He was looking for an investment crop to plant on property he owned in Southold. Listening to their plans, he settled on grapes. He began helping out at the Hargrave vineyard, learning with them and arranging to buy some of the vines they had ordered for the next year, enough to plant one acre at Southold in 1974. Mudd had no interest in starting a winery: "Winemaking is laboratory work and that's not for me."

Over the next three years Mudd and his son Steve planted 26 acres of mixed vinifera varieties. It was a leap of faith. They would soon have more than 50 tons of grapes to sell with no obvious buyers in sight. The only local winery was a strictly estate-grown operation and there were few other wineries for hundreds of miles.

Their timing, however, proved prescient. One month after their latest vines went into the ground New York passed its Farm Winery Law, smoothing the way for Long Island wine entrepreneurs. At the same time, Suffolk County began implementing an innovative farmland preservation program designed to slow the loss of Long Island's open lands to housing and commercial development. It offered farmers a cash payment in exchange for development rights, a legally binding commitment embedded in deeds to keep farms open. The land would then be sellable, for agriculture, for less than market value to developers.

The county started purchasing development rights in 1977, hoping to give potato farmers the financial ability to switch to another crop. Instead they began selling their development rights and then selling their farms, mostly to buyers from out of the area who had read about wine vineyards going in on Long Island.

Cornell's cooperative extension agent in Suffolk County, a vegetable specialist also intrigued by the prospects for wine, planted a mini-demonstration vineyard at the Riverhead research station, and started organizing twilight meetings at the Hargrave and Mudd vineyards in the late 1970s, for aspiring growers. The Mudds began helping to prep fields and get vines planted for newcomers, often absentee owners. In 1980 father and son officially launched a consulting, installation, and management business: Mudd Vineyards Ltd. In six years they had become the resident experts. Steve Mudd later allowed: "For the first ten years-plus quite honestly no one had a clue of how to go about it and do it properly," resulting in some "bad wine."

The root problem was, in fact, a problem associated with vine roots. East End soils were fiercely acidic for grapes—especially European varieties—with pH values between 4.0 and 5.0 disrupting vine functions. At the same time grapevines were sucking up residual nitrogen from soil heavily fertilized for potatoes, sending 30-foot branches flying down trellises and massing dense foliage that led to problems ripening fruit. Growers needed to realign their vineyards onto de-vigorating rootstocks, then simply, agonizingly, wait for soils to lose their nitrogen buzz.

Then there were problems above ground. In a 2003 memoir, Louisa Hargrave laid much of the blame for Long Island's flailing viticultural debut at the feet of Cornell viticulturist Nelson Shaulis, for advising growers to trellis their vines as if they were the Concords of upstate, a training system hostile to vinifera. Shaulis was an internationally respected scientist with a stubborn blind spot about growing vinifera in his home state. He had actually planted a research block of Riesling at the Geneva Experiment Station back in the 1950s but he still hewed to the antique station policy that European varieties were too risky for New York. At his retirement in the early 1980s Shaulis was replaced by California-native Bob Pool, who promptly wrote a pamphlet on "Growing Vinifera Grapes on Long Island." He would put research at the Geneva Experiment Station on a more progressive track. In any case, virtually all Long Island vineyards would be planted with vinifera: 1,600 acres in the first ten years, more than half set in the ground by the Mudd consulting company.

One of the Mudds's first customers, Peter and Patricia Lenz, owned a trendy Westhampton Beach restaurant called A Moveable Feast until, as they described it, the challenge was gone. In 1978 they sold the restaurant, bought land in Peconic, hired the Mudds to plant a new challenge and Hargrave-winemaker Kleck to pull it off. Air traffic controller Ray Blum was one of the next on the scene when Ronald Reagan rendered him unemployed. Blum put in 17 acres at Peconic Bay Vineyards in 1979.

A Stony Brook physician named Herodotus Damianos hired the Mudds to establish Pindar Vineyards next door to Lenz. Pindar quickly became the island's largest investment in grapes: nearly 100 acres planted in three years. The winery jump-started with a wine made from Finger Lakes French hybrid grapes, a semi-sweet crowd-pleaser for early cash flow. It was an anomaly; Long Island wine would grow up virtually untouched by hybrid (or native) varieties and with little input from upstate apart from Cornell.

Most of the newcomers contracted with the Mudds or hired farm managers and winemakers. The owner of a fuel-oil business in Nassau County, Kip Bedell, chose instead the purple-hands approach. With the experience of one harvest at the Hargrave farm but many years as a serious home winemaker, he bought 50-acres in Peconic and started planting Merlot. Like the Hargraves he was most interested in the prospect of New York's first red wine district. Still, during the first decade, nearly half the vineyard acreage on the East End was planted in Chardonnay; these were the years when California Chardonnay mesmerized the American wine market.

There were persuasive reasons for vineyard investors to favor the North over the South Fork: lower land prices and development pressure above all, but also somewhat more consistent soils, a bit less exposure to the brunt of Atlantic storms, and a surprisingly longer growing season. The first two ventures on the South Fork both failed. With more careful site selection a smaller community of wineries gradually took root, including some satellite operations of North Fork growers.

There was one Long Island outlier, growing wine in Nassau County just 22 miles from Manhattan. The Banfi importing firm, purveyors of Italian and Chilean wines, planted 60 acres of Chardonnay on the estate of their Old Brookville corporate headquarters in the early 1980s. They hired Fred Frank, Konstantin's grandson, to manage the vineyard and make Banfi Gold Coast Chardonnay at the Frank winery facilities upstate. The interior island location of the vineyard—plagued by spring frosts—proved the wisdom of putting grapes out on the East End; yields were disappointing. Banfi's winegrowing venture ultimately dwindled to a remnant vineyard decorating the estate.

Long Island's total vineyard acreage swelled rapidly through the 80s, to the point where the grape crop overwhelmed the capacity of the island's new wineries. Chardonnay in particular was in serious oversupply. By the end of the decade grapes and juice were an Island export, giving a vinifera boost to wineries in Connecticut, the Hudson Valley and the Finger Lakes—reversing the old commerce of upstate fruit to downstate (urban) wineries. As East End wineries grew and many more opened through the 90s, supply and demand came into better balance. This was helped along by a service started by Russell Hearn, the winemaker at Pellegrini Vineyards. His contract production facility, the Premium Wine Group, handled everything from crush through fermentation and aging to bottling, for start-ups or winery expansions. In its first year it processed more than 500 tons. It would do for Island wineries what Mudd had done 20 years earlier for vineyards.

A symposium held in 1988 called "Bring Bordeaux to Long Island" formalized the inclination of winegrowers to look toward France for models and mentors. High-profile French winemakers and international researchers came to the island to explore similarities between Bordeaux and the East End. A follow-up conference two years later narrowed the focus to the variety Merlot.

As East End wine entered its third decade, one wine blogger noted that "an increasingly popular thing to plant alongside a winery was a 'For Sale' sign." The outposts of pioneers fermenting grapes in potato barns had become valuable properties in the East Coast's stellar new wine region. Liaisons with Chateaux Margaux and Pichon-Lalande gave East End wine a bit of the luster of Medoc royalty. The Francophile New York City market, initially dismissive or dubious at best, came around to cheering on its own local wine. The next step after buying the wine became buying the wineries.

FIGURE 9.2. Raphael Vineyards was one of the most ambitious new ventures when Long Island winemaking jumped up from its potato-barn period in the '90s. The $6 million, timber-frame winery was modeled after Tuscan monasteries, atop a 12-foot-deep cellar. The barrel room was not only outfitted with French oak cooperage, it was constructed with French oak. The managing director of Chateau Margaux, Paul Pontalier, consulted. (*Courtesy of Raphael Winery*)

In July 1999 a group of American and Chilean investors bought the small Laurel Lake Vineyards winery near Mattituck for $2 million. A few months later the Hargraves sold their iconic wine estate to investors led by an expatriate Italian count for almost $4 million. In another few months a Hollywood film producer paid $5 million for Bedell Cellars. The number of millions kept climbing with more turnovers and more investors establishing new estates.

Such an infusion of big money was familiar in California but new to New York, and not happening elsewhere in the state. Long Island vineyards lost their ragged edges; they became increasingly manicured, viticultural showpieces. Cellars could afford the latest technology, the finest French barrels. Absentee owners hired talent from a small group of experienced East End winemakers; each of them might oversee the production at half a dozen different wineries, a kind of winemaker franchise system that imprinted Long Island wines with both technical competence and a degree of stylistic uniformity. The exclusive focus on vinifera varieties and the relatively uniform *terroir* of vineyards across the East End—in topography, soils, climate—had already put a consistent stamp on the wines that was unique in New York.

For such a young wine district, Long Island seemed remarkably mature. At least New-World mature.

CHAPTER 10

Diaspora

The challenge now is to grow the market at a greater rate than winery growth, so that new wineries aren't cannibalizing the market share of pioneers who got everything started in the first place.

—James Trezise, New York Wine & Grape Foundation

During the first decade of the twenty-first century nearly 200 new wineries opened in New York State, and the rate at which they appeared was continuing to accelerate. There had been 19 wineries when the Farm Winery Law passed in 1976. In 2010 there were more than 300.

The Finger Lakes and Long Island regions experienced the most growth but wineries were cropping up all over the state, in 50 of its 62 counties. Commercial winemaking proliferated in an arc around the perimeter of the state, from the Pennsylvania border in Chautauqua County north along the shores of Lakes Erie and Ontario to the Thousand Islands region of the St. Lawrence River, east to the valley of Lake Champlain, down the Hudson River Valley to Long Island and, ultimately, New York City. New York wine became more diverse, more promising, more impressive, more inconsistent, more fractured and confusing than ever.

Finger Lakes

Viticulture had begun to spread out from Keuka and Canandaigua Lakes in the nineteenth century but winemaking stayed rooted there until much later. As French hybrid and especially vinifera varieties settled in, the locus of winemaking shifted east to the lower elevations, milder temperatures, and less acidic soils of the bigger lakes, Seneca and Cayuga. After Gold Seal planted 120 acres of Riesling and Chardonnay on the southeast shore of Seneca Lake in the 1970s, that slope became the new center point of Finger Lakes wine, nicknamed "the banana belt" for its reputation as the region's warmest microclimate. By 2010 there were 22 wineries and several hundred vineyard acres along a 12-mile stretch of lakeshore from Hector to Lodi. The extent of vineyards approached what it had been a century earlier.

Most of the new Finger Lakes vineyards were being planted to vinifera varieties: Riesling above all; smaller commitments to Gewurztraminer, Pinot Gris, Pinot Blanc, and Grunerveltliner. Wineries began routinely making Chardonnay in both stainless-steel and barrel-fermented versions. The region's tradition as a white wine district continued, but the trend of warmer, longer growing seasons and a run of healthy publicity for red wine led to increased planting of Pinot Noir, Lemberger, and especially Cabernet Franc. Those warmer seasons from climate change left some winemakers (not grape growers) worrying less about getting Riesling ripe and more about getting it too ripe, fattening up and losing its acid edge.

While they grabbed most of the attention in wine magazines, European varieties continued to fill only a small percentage of the region's wine tanks. A 150-year legacy of viticulture still surrounded the lakes and inhabited most tasting sheets. Some listed dozens of wines made from a staggering assortment of grape species and varieties.

Among the native Americans, Catawba, Concord, and Delaware prevailed, but a number of wineries kept alive a deeper archive of the region's heritage: Diamond, Isabella, Iona, Vergennes, Ives. By the 1990s growers and winemakers were sorting out winners and losers among the two dozen French hybrid varieties introduced since the 1930s. Aurora, Chelois, Chancellor, and deChaunac were falling by the wayside. Baco Noir, Marechal Foch, and Seyval Blanc became standards. Vignoles and Vidal Blanc emerged as the standouts, particularly for late-harvest and ice wines and adopted even by wineries committed to vinifera.

The introduction of Cayuga White in 1972 breathed new life into the Geneva Experiment Station's 100-year-old grape breeding program. It produced the Finger Lakes own *vin de pays* and ushered in more hybrids bred for New York vineyards: Traminette, Noiret, Corot Noir, and several seedless table grapes.

The ballooning array of Finger Lakes wines led some winemakers to organize focus groups. Half a dozen producers committed to dry, vinifera wines formed a Finger Lakes Wine Guild in 2005, linking members by wine style rather than by lake. Skeptical colleagues dubbed it "the vinifera mafia." The Finger Lakes Pinot Noir Alliance made another attempt to focus in on a chaotic landscape of labels. One winery alone, Chateau Frank, carried on the tradition of specializing in sparkling wine. Some winemakers worried that the Finger Lakes appellation, just gaining recognition in uber-wine circles, was getting Balkanized by wine trails drawing promotional borders around each lake. Identifying communes within the larger region might be a logical step in maturing a young wine district if they were based on *terroir*, not tourism.

The appearance of more and better dry, food-oriented wines helped inspire a progressive local food scene promoted by the umbrella group Finger Lakes Culinary Bounty: thriving small farms, back-road cheese dairies, savvy restaurants—sure signs of a ripening wine district. Another sign: single-vineyard designations on labels, as winemakers began identifying exceptional micro-sites and their varietal expressions and affinities.

Chautauqua–Erie

At the outset of the twenty-first century two-thirds of New York State's 33,000 acres of vineyards lined a 30-mile stretch of Lake Erie shoreline, the largest concentration of grapevines in the United States outside California. Ninety-five percent of those vines were Concords, supplying much of the world with grape juice and jelly. In 2010 barely a dozen wineries operated in the long shadow of Welch Foods.

Naturally nearly all of them made wine from Concord grapes, and from other native varieties. Mogen David was still a major player in the kosher wine market. The Johnson Estate had brought French hybrids to the area in the 1960s and Woodbury Vineyards, early cooperators with Konstantin Frank, introduced vinifera in the 1970s, but the entrenched culture of the Grape Belt kept Concord king and wine varieties a fringe crop. To fill out their lists most wineries bought hybrid and vinifera grapes and wine from the Finger Lakes and Long Island.

Chautauqua–Erie was the only New York region with fewer wineries at the start of the twenty-first century than it had in the nineteenth.

Niagara Escarpment

A 2002 study commissioned by New York's Department of Agriculture & Markets identified the southwestern rim of Lake Ontario as the state's most promising undeveloped region for viniculture. It referenced Cornell data on climate, topography, and soils specifically along the escarpment ridge paralleling the lake shore between the Niagara River and Orleans County.

Focusing on the escarpment was key to realizing the district's potential. Lake Ontario's southern shore had a long history of orchard culture with second-fiddle grapevines too often relegated to inferior sites on the plain between escarpment and lake. When the Taylor Company cut loose many of its contract growers in the 1970s, poorly-drained, underachieving Niagara County vineyards were among the first to go.

When orchards ran into tough economic times in the 1990s, the absence of entrenched viticulture proved to be an asset; it gave the area a fresh start. Hybrid and vinifera vineyards began spreading along the ridge line. Niagara Landing Wine Cellars opened in 1998, the first of more than 15 wineries clustering around the old Erie Canal town of Lockport within a dozen years.

The most ambitious start-up was the brainchild of engineer-turned-Pinot-Noir-fanatic Michael von Heckler. After meticulous site research—studies that earned the Niagara Escarpment its official appellation—von Heckler began planting, exclusively, the most challenging of wine grapes on the slope west of Lockport. In a few years he lined up investors to expand the vineyard to 55 acres. It was the largest block of Pinot Noir in the United States outside the West Coast, matched to a winery full of expensive French cooperage. Warm Lake Estate became the emblem of a vibrant new wine district. Its shooting star arced through half a dozen uneven vintages, then flamed out in foreclosure, a textbook case of overreach.

Owners of nearby Freedom Run Winery bought the Warm Lake property at auction in 2010, turned the winery into an art studio and set about rescuing neglected vines. In that year the region of the Niagara Escarpment had about 400 acres of vineyard.

Thousand Islands

Near where the St. Lawrence River drains Lake Ontario, retiring Army Captain Steve Conaway returned to Fort Drum after tours of duty in Afghanistan and in Germany, where he had discovered wine. With images of the Rhine River Valley fresh on his mind, he looked at Boldt Castle on its island in the St. Lawrence and thought "where are the vineyards?"

Conaway bought a dairy farm near Alexandria Bay and planted a trial of more than a dozen wine-grape varieties. Thirty-below temperatures and withering winds off Lake Ontario soon winnowed his collection down to a few ultra-hardy hybrids bred in Minnesota. They had recently made wine-grape growing feasible in the upper Midwest and they would do the same in New York's North Country. He ran a tiny ad in the local newspaper: "[I]nterested in growing grapes? . . . let's get together." The response was surprising. Soon a small band of enthusiasts was peppering the countryside between the river and Tug Hill Plateau with Minnesota-hybrid grapevines, varieties entirely new to New York—Frontenac, LaCrescent, Brianna, Marquette. One grower started a nursery: Seaway Cold-Hardy Grapevines.

Conaway's Thousand Island Winery opened in 2004, followed by half a dozen more in as many years. While they all signed on to the goal of creating wines with a different pedigree from anything else in New York, most of them bought juice from the Finger Lakes and Long Island to jump-start sales. Conaway's location near the resort town of Alex Bay gave Thousand Islands Winery a leg up for rapid growth; in five years it was making 30,000 gallons, but only 10 percent from local grapes. There were 80 acres of vineyards in northwestern Jefferson County in 2010. It would take plenty of grit and layers of long underwear to sustain the resolve to develop truly regional wine.

Champlain Valley

The same can be said of the North Country's other budding wine district. Winegrowing around Lake Champlain grew out of the locavore movement in Vermont in the 1990s, spreading to New York's side of the lake ten years later. Orchardists and small-fruit growers took their cue from colleagues in the Thousand Islands area and started experimenting with Minnesota hybrid grapes.

Fruit-growing on Lake Champlain was as old as European settlement, when French-Canadians planted apple orchards in the 1700s for table fruit and hard cider. Grapes also had a surprising history here. Two varieties grown for Finger Lakes wine in the 1800s originated in Champlain gardens: Vergennes, from the Vermont village south of Burlington, and the Adirondac grape, a chance cross-breed discovered in a Port Henry backyard.

The Adirondack massif looming west of the valley wrings moisture out of weather moving east off the Great Lakes, leaving Champlain farms relatively dry and sunny. A potentially short season and deep winter freezes were the limiting factors for viticulture. Local growers got a boost in 2005 when Cornell University added cold-hardy grape trials to its Baker Research Farm in Willsboro. The 25 varieties planted included Minnesota hybrids, older French hybrids and the latest crosses from the Geneva Experiment Station, testing their viability in the region but also serving as a reference vineyard and training ground for area farmers.

By 2012 there were nearly a dozen micro-vineyards and wineries on New York's side of the lake, clustered along its wide, deep, northern basin.

Hudson Valley

A number of fruit-growers scattered through the hills south of Lake Champlain organized the Upper Hudson Valley Wine & Grape Association in 2010, a clearinghouse for exchanging ideas and experience in uplands between the state's newest and oldest wine districts. The name had a wistful ring to it; the area lay well beyond the benefits from a maritime climate carried up-river.

In the lower valley, Marlboro-winemaker Mark Miller's vision of vineyards someday enveloping the Hudson River, "an American Cote d'Or," had begun to falter in his own time. His involvement in an overheated scheme to develop large vineyards on the river nearly sank the Benmarl winery in the mid-1970s. The proximity to New York City, once a boon to farms along the river, eventually created a real estate market too pricey for vineyards. The creep of development that smothered High Tor Vineyards in the 70s kept moving north, unchecked by the kind of development-rights program protecting agriculture on Long Island's East End.

Farm wineries proliferated, but most were pushed back from the river into turbulent terrain and microclimates that complicated choosing where and what to plant. Viticulture was essentially just getting started in the Hudson Valley; there were almost no vineyards left from the old days; the last of Brotherhood's had become a parking lot. Even most of Benmarl's vineyard was run-down and needed replanting by new owners.

New plantings were small-scale. Millbrook Vineyards' 32 acres was the region's largest, established in the 80s by New York's former Commissioner of Commerce John Dyson, a key player in passage of the Farm Winery Law and generous backer of research at the Geneva Experiment Station. A fan of Konstantin Frank, Dyson planted his vineyard entirely with vinifera varieties; unusual for the area. Novices confronting the uncertainties of Hudson Valley terrain inclined toward hardier, more forgiving hybrids. Given the region's farming tradition, wines were also routinely made from many fruits other than grapes, most often apples but increasingly from black currants.

The disheartening history and inherent challenges of grapes in the valley added up to about 500 acres of vineyards in 2010, where 130 years earlier there had been 13,000. Those 500 acres constituted the most dispersed official viticultural area in New York, cleaved by the river into three scattered wine trails. The selection of wines was also the most diverse in the state. With over 40 wineries drawing from only 500 acres, there needed to be substantial imports of grapes from the Finger Lakes, Long Island, and beyond. In this regard New York's oldest viticultural district looked something like its newest. The Brotherhood Winery was making close to a million cases of wine with nearly three dozen different labels but only three of them carried a Hudson Valley appellation. The Royal Kedem Winery in Milton, the valley's largest, bought all its fruit from Lake Erie and the Finger Lakes. Nearly all of the farm wineries also augmented their small vineyards with out-of-region grapes.

Where Hudson wineries looked most progressive was in "green" building design and innovative cellars. Several wineries were relying on solar or wind-generated electricity and using geothermal heating systems. Stoutridge Vineyard in Marlboro designed a hillside, gravity-flow cellar warmed with heat recirculated from their own distillery.

Long Island

The early investment of Long Island winegrowers in Cabernet Sauvignon, Merlot, and Chardonnay began to yield, after the first decades, to a restless interest in other options. Sauvignon Blanc, which had produced some promising wines early on before running into viticultural snags, started blossoming as vineyard skills improved. More wineries began making sparkling wine and rosé. The Albarino grape of Spain's Atlantic Galicia province looked like a good bet for the maritime East End. Led by the South Fork's Channing Daughters Winery, growers were probing the island's lighter side, acknowledging that even the dangling East End was still attached, however tenuously, to the rest of cool-climate New York.

As for the Island's iconic Merlot, as good as it got, some critics began asking if, in Long Island's sandy soil, it would ever approach the stature of Merlot grown in clay-veined Pomerol. Winemakers got more serious about blending Merlot with other Bordeaux varieties, notably Cabernet Franc and Malbec.

Chardonnay remained by far the most widely grown of Long Island's white wine grapes. It easily fell into a regional style of taut fruit and minimal oak, shaped for seafood. The wine-food connection, particularly the restaurant connection, grew stronger on the East End than anywhere else in the state. Chefs and restaurateurs were occasionally turning into winemakers.

The sustainable farming movement also took hold here more readily than upstate. It began with concerns about the Island's vulnerable aquifer. Vineyards adopted state-of-the-art recycling sprayers and spray-rig cleaning stations. Certified organic viticulture had started in the Finger Lakes (Four Chimneys Farm Winery, Barrington Cellars, and Silver Thread Vineyard), but they proved to be regional outliers. When Cornell University's extension program eventually took an interest and created a workbook outlining how the state's growers could transition to more sustainable practices, Long Islanders decided the standards were too weak and wrote their own plan. The challenges of going organic in a humid climate made full certification difficult, but most growers adopted at least some aspects of organic culture, led by Macari and Shinn Estate.

The turnover of winery ownerships at prices approaching Napa Valley numbers highlighted financial challenges. Escalating real estate values, with or without development rights, tested the economic viability of growing grapes. The spread of vineyards slowed on the North Fork and stalled amid the fancy estates of the South Fork's Hamptons. Price tags on Long Island wines reflected the economic pressures; they often approached twice the price of a comparable bottle from the Finger Lakes. With no plantings of higher-yielding, lower-input hybrids or native varieties, there was no backstop of more affordable wines. High prices could fly at winery tasting rooms much more easily than out in the marketplace.

Some island winemakers were in the business to make a living but they were working in an environment where wealthy folks like Robert Entenmann, heir to a bakery fortune, could indulge their whims: "I looked around and everybody was planting a vineyard. It looked like it would be fun." Entenmann's Martha Clara Vineyard became one of the North Fork's showcase wine estates. The vision of a region taking its cues from stellar Bordeaux chateaux was becoming more complicated.

New York City

New recipes for making wine appeared in New York City with the twenty-first century, mixing in various ingredients of street-theater, music, visual arts and, of course, food. Manhattan's City Winery opened in 2007 with glass walls allowing folks walking down Varick

Street or zipping by in taxis to glimpse into the bowels of a working wine cellar, or watch lugs of grapes being dumped onto sidewalk sorting tables. The facility was designed to produce its own house-wine for an on-site restaurant, tasting room, and concert hall, but also to work with an urban underground of would-be winemakers. They could select a grape variety, a vineyard source, the type of oak barrel, and play whatever roll they might choose in the drama of producing their own wine (all for what would end up costing close to $30 a bottle).

It was a city winery but not exactly a *New York* city winery. Nearly all the grapes were trucked in from high-profile West Coast vineyards or flown in from South America. Manhattan was still looking past its backyard to trade on the world stage. New urban wineries were starting up in Brooklyn with a more locavore approach. One of them, Brooklyn Oenology, folded winemaking into a gallery and studio in Williamsburg where local artists designed BOE's labels around themes of the state's agricultural, culinary and visual arts. Grapes came entirely from Finger Lakes and Long Island vineyards.

On Brooklyn's less-hipster bay side, Red Hook Winery turned more to the mechanics. It contracted for grapes from over a dozen vineyards on the East End and Seneca Lake. Two California-trained winemakers, one with a technical approach, the other a free-wheeling experimenter, signed on to work with an across-the-state sampling of New York *terroir*. They divided each batch of grapes from each vineyard and worked independently with often wildly different results, giving tasters a wide-angle look at the magical transmutation of grapes into wine.

A *New York Times* columnist wrote: "I've had some Schoener [the experimenter] wines that I would rather think about than drink;" a comment that merits pondering in its own right. It is good to keep in mind that wine, for all its intricacies, is at heart a drink in the service of food; but wine has also always invited and inspired a special kind of freed-up contemplation, a line of thinking that can explore geography, weave it into art and culture, drift into the future or back in time. Red Hook's location was only a couple of miles from the site of Andre Parmentier's and Alden Spooner's seminal experiments with winegrowing two centuries earlier. They were grandfathers of everything that came after. In the intervening years the urge to make wine roamed all over the state, to all its extremities, coming full circle back to the mouth of the Hudson River.

Red Hook's geography also put it squarely in the crosshairs of Hurricane Sandy, thrashing the winery to within an inch of its life with a climate message that gives winegrowers and wine drinkers everywhere much to think about. The decades ahead may make the challenges of the past—the insects, cold winters, dumb laws, diseases, even the storms—seem tame. For all its struggles and transformations, against the backdrop of the world of wine, New York's story has just begun.

Timeline

c. 20,000 BC   Southern terminus of Wisconsin glacial advance deposits Long Island after scouring the Hudson Valley.

c. 15,000 BC   Receding glacial moraine blocks river valleys, ultimately forming Finger Lakes.

1524   Giovanni da Verrazzano describes wild grapevines on his exploration of the North American coastline.

1609   Henry Hudson sails up the North River, trading trinkets for grapes with friendly natives.

1615   Samuel de Champlain observes grapevines on an expedition into Iroquois country.

Early 1600s   Wine made from European variety grapes at New Mexico missions.

1621   Wine made from wild grapes at Plymouth Colony's first Thanksgiving.

1642   European grapevines planted at Rensselaerswyck in upper Hudson Valley, unsuccessfully.

1660s   Jesuit missionaries in Iroquois country make wine for mass from wild grapes.

c. 1750   William Prince establishes America's first commercial nursery, including grapevines, in Flushing.

1808	A Glens Falls physician forms the nation's first local temperance organization.
1820s	Alphonse Loubat and Andre Parmentier attempt to grow and disseminate European vinifera grapevines in Brooklyn, unsuccessfully.
1824	James Monier plants Isabella and Catawba vines in his Naples garden.
	Elijah Fay plants the same grapes beside his Brocton cabin.
1827	Robert Underhill replants a failed vinifera vineyard on Croton Point with Catawba and Isabella grapes, New York's first successful commercial vineyard.
1830	William Robert Prince publishes A Treatise on the Vine, the early bible of New World grape culture.
	Reverend William Bostwick plants Isabella and Catawba vines in his Hammondsport rectory garden and begins disseminating cuttings.
1836	Samuel Warren advertises his sacramental York Wines in the Genesee Valley, the commercial debut of wine in New York State.
1839	After trying to sell table grapes, John Jaques opens a winery in Washingtonville.
1847	Lawyer Edward McKay establishes the Canandaigua Lake region's first tiny commercial vineyard in Naples.
1852	The Ada grape, bred in Flushing, becomes the first deliberate European-American hybrid grape variety to enter commercial channels.
	Andrew Reisinger introduces German viticultural practices to the Finger Lakes.
1857	The first commercial wine enterprise in the Finger Lakes, Highland Cottage, lasts only a few vintages.

1859	Partners found Brocton Wine Cellars, the Chautauqua–Erie region's first winery.
1860	Pleasant Valley Wine Company becomes the first successful Finger Lakes winery.
1861	Banker Hiram Maxfield opens the first winery in the Canandaigua Lake region, at Naples.
1873	The Woman's Christian Temperance Union (WCTU) is conceived at the Chautauqua Institution.
1882	A cooper, Walter Taylor, establishes the Taylor Wine Company.
	New York State opens an agricultural experiment station in Geneva.
1888	Swiss immigrant Jacob Widmer launches Widmer's Wine Cellars in Naples.
1890	New York State has overtaken Ohio to become second in wine production after California.
1902	Experimental planting of European vinifera grapevines at the Geneva Experiment Station.
1907	Publication of *The Grapes of New York* by U. P. Hedrick and co-authors.
1912	Paul Garrett brings his national wine enterprise to New York at Penn Yan.
1920	The 18th Amendment to the Constitution imposes national Prohibition.
1933	The 21st Constitutional Amendment repeals national Prohibition.
1934	French Champagne-maker Charles Fournier hired to rehabilitate the Urbana Wine Company.
Mid-1930s	First commercial vineyard of French hybrid grapevines outside France, planted on Keuka Lake.

1944	Canandaigua Industries opens in an abandoned sauer-kraut plant.
1953	High Tor Vineyards becomes the first small, farm-based winery in New York since Prohibition.
	Konstantin Frank hired to grow vinifera grapes at Gold Seal Vineyards.
	Canandaigua Industries launches Richard's Wild Irish Rose.
1959	First commercial vintage from vinifera grapes in the eastern U.S., at Gold Seal Vineyards.
1961	Widmer family sells Widmer's Wine Cellars to investors.
	Taylor Wine Company becomes a public corporation, takes over Pleasant Valley Wine Company.
1962	First vintage at Konstantin Frank's Vinifera Wine Cellars.
1963	European vinifera grape culture successfully introduced to Long Island at Wickham Farms in Cutchogue.
1970	Fired from Taylor Wine Company, Walter S. Taylor establishes Bully Hill Vineyards at original family homestead.
1971	Mark Miller opens Benmarl Vineyards winery in Marlboro.
1972	The Geneva Agricultural Experiment Station releases its first grape variety bred specifically for wine: Cayuga White.
1973	Louisa and Alexander Hargrave plant Long Island's first vinifera wine vineyard.
1976	Governor Hugh Carey signs New York Farm Winery Law, initiating a renaissance of small wineries.
1977	Coca-Cola Company acquires the Taylor Wine Company.

1979	Seagram Company acquires Gold Seal Vineyards.
1983	Seagram purchases Taylor Wine from Coca-Cola, closes historic Gold Seal winery.
1985	Seagram cancels all Taylor and Gold Seal contracts with grape growers.
	State legislation creates the New York Wine & Grape Foundation to support research and promotion.
1986	Canandaigua Wine Company buys Widmer's Wine Cellars.
1993	Canandaigua Wine Company acquires the Taylor, Great Western and Gold Seal brands; becomes America's second largest wine producer.
1998	Niagara Landing Wine Cellars rekindles winegrowing on Lake Ontario
2004	Commercial winemaking comes to New York's North Country at Thousand Islands Winery.
2008	A new iteration of the urban winery appears in Manhattan and Brooklyn.

Surviving Nineteenth-Century Winery Structures

Around three dozen nineteenth-century New York wineries still existed in one form or another in the early years of the twenty-first century, some as ongoing wine businesses, some in ruins, many in all manner of different iterations. The list here is probably incomplete.

Hudson Valley

Brotherhood Wine Co.—In operation.

Croton Point Wine Vaults—Abandoned but preserved (on park property).

Hudson Valley Wine Co.—Abandoned.

Schapiro Wine Company—Cellars under lower Manhattan's Rivington Street.

Hammondsport/Pleasant Valley

Columbia Wine Co.—In operation (part of Pleasant Valley Wine Co.).

Connolly Brothers Winery—Abandoned.

Freidell Winery—Used for storage.

Germania Wine Cellars—Abandoned.

Haase Rheims Wine Cellars—Private residence.

McCorn Wine Co.—Private residence.

Monarch Wine Co—In renovation.

Old Monastery Wine Co.—Abandoned.

Pleasant Valley Wine Co.—In operation.

Rheims Valley Wine Co.—Private residence.

Roualet Winery—Abandoned.

Vine City Wine Co.—Used for storage.

Keuka Lake

Eckel's Wine Cellar—Private residence.

Pulteney Wine Co.—In ruins.

Rose Winery—Private residence.

Taylor Wine Co.—Renovated as Bully Hill Vineyards restaurant.

Urbana Wine Co.—Abandoned.

Western New York Wine Co.—In operation as Chateau Frank.

White Top Champagne Co.—Used for storage.

Seneca Lake

Seneca Lake Wine Co.—In ruins.

Naples/Canandaigua Lake

Graff Wine Cellars—Abandoned but preserved.

Maxfield Wine Cellars—Part of Lake Country Woodworkers.

Miller Winery—Private residence.

Widmer's Wine Cellars—In operation as Hazlitt's Red Cat Cellars.

Hemlock Lake

O-Neh-Da Winery—In operation as Eagle Crest Vineyards.

Bath

McCormick Wine Co.—Auto parts store.

Western New York

Henry Card Winery—Part survives as a Fredonia furniture store.

Irondequoit Wine Co.—Part of original building encased within a modern business.

John Michael Winery—Private Dansville residence.

Lake Erie and Missouri Wine Co. (Harris community)—Abandoned beehive cellars.

Samuel Warren Winery—Museum of Town of York Historical Society.

Sources

Adams, Leon D., *The Wines of America*, 4th edition. New York: McGraw-Hill, 1990.

Beers, F. W., *Atlases of New York Counties*. New York: Beers, 1872.

Bishop, J. Leander, *A History of American Manufactures*. Philadelphia: Young, 1861.

Bunnell, A. O., *Dansville Historical Biographical Descriptive: 1789–1902*. Dansville: Instructor, 1905.

Burroughs, John, *Leaf and Tendril*. Boston: Houghton, Mifflin, 1908.

Carfizzi, Joseph A., *History of the Lower Hudson Valley Before the Revolution*. Wallkill: Carfizzi, 2005.

Cattell, Hudson, and H. Lee Stauffer, *The Wines of the East*. Lancaster: L & H Photojournalism, 1978–80.

Chazanof, William, *Welch's Grape Juice: From Corporation to Cooperative*. Syracuse: Syracuse Univ. Press, 1977

Chidsey, Donald Barr, *On and Off the Wagon*. New York: Cowles, 1969.

Clayton, W. Woodward, *History of Steuben County*. Higginson, 1879.

Crissey, S. S., ed., *Chautauqua Fruits, Grapes and Grape Products*. Dunkirk: Dunkirk Co., 1901.

Crosby, Everett, *The Vintage Years*. New York: Harper & Row, 1973.

Cuthbert, Arthur, *The Life and Work of Thomas Lake Harris*. New York: AMS Press, 1909.

Danckaerts, Jasper, *Journal of Jasper Danckaerts (1679)*. L. I. Historical Society, 1867.

Denniston, Goldsmith, *Grape Culture in Steuben County*. Albany: Van Benthuysen, 1865.

Denton, Daniel, *A Brief Description of New York (1670)*. New York: Gowans, 1845.

181

Disturnell, J., A *Gazetteer of the State of New York*. Albany: Van Benthuysen, 1843–73.

Emerson, Edward. R., *The Story of the Vine*. New York: Putnam's, 1902.

Furman, Gabriel, *Notes, Geographical and Historical, Relating to the Town of Brooklyn on Long Island (1824)*. Online <UNL.edu>.

Gordon, William Reed, *Keuka Lake Memories: the Champagne Country, 1835–1935*. Interlaken: Heart of the Lakes, 1986.

Grant, W. L., ed., *Voyages of Samuel de Champlain: 1604–1618*. New York: Scribner, 1907.

Hargrave, Louisa Thomas, *The Vineyard*. New York: Penguin, 2003.

Hedrick, Ulysses P., *The Grapes of New York*. Albany: J. B. Lyon, 1908.

———. *Manual of American Grape Growing*. New York: MacMillan, 1919.

———. *A History of Agriculture in the State of New York*. 1933.

Huggett, Jennifer M. "Geology and Wine: A Review." *Proceedings of the Geologists' Association* 117 (2006).

Husmann, George, *American Grape Growing and Wine Making*. New York: Orange Judd, 1880.

Isachsen, Y. I. ed., et al., *The Geology of New York*. Albany: New York State Museum, 1991.

Juet, Robert, *Journal of Henry Hudson 1609 Expedition*. Purchas His Pilgrimes, 1625.

Kammen, Michael, *Colonial New York, A History*. New York: Scribner's, 1975.

Loubat, Alphonse, *The American Vine-Dresser's Guide*. New York: Carvill, 1827.

Martell, Alan R., and Alton Long, *The Wines and Wineries of the Hudson Valley*. Woodstock, VT: Countryman, 1993.

McPhee, John, *Annals of the Former World*. New York: Farrar, Straus and Giroux, 1998.

Mendelson, Richard, *From Demon to Darling: A Legal History of Wine in America*. Berkeley: Univ. of California, 2009.

Miller, John, *New York Considered and Improved (1695)*. New York: Paltsits.

Miller, Mark, *Wine–A Gentleman's Game*. New York: Harper & Row, 1984.

Miller, William J., *The Geological History of New York State*. Pt. Washington: Kennikat, 1914.

Mitzky, C., *Our Native Grape: Grapes and their Culture*. Rochester: Mitzky, 1893.

Morris, G. H., "Rise of the Grape and Wine Industry in the Naples Valley" MA thesis, Syracuse University, 1955.

O'Callaghan, Edmund B., *The Documentary History of the State of New York*. Albany: Weed, Parsons, 1849–51.

Okrent, Daniel, *Last Call: The Rise and Fall of Prohibition*. New York: Scribner, 2010.

Palmanteer, Mabel, *The Grape and Wine Industry of Naples, NY*. 1936.

Palmedo, Philip, and Edward Beltrami, *The Wines of Long Island: Birth of a Region*. Richmond: Waterline, 1993.

Peck, William F., *History of Rochester and Monroe County*. New York: Pioneer, 1908.

Pegram, Thomas R., *Battling Demon Rum: The Struggle for a Dry America, 1800–1933*. 1998.

Pinney, Thomas, *A History of Wine in America: From the Beginnings to Prohibition*. Berkeley: Univ. of California, 1989.

———. *A History of Wine in America: From Prohibition to the Present*. 2005.

Prince, William R., *A Treatise on the Vine*. New York: Swords, 1830.

Ross, John, *The Story of North Fork Wine*. Huntington: Maple Hill Press, 2009.

Sands, Richard, and Rob Sands, *Reaching for the Stars: The Making of Constellation Brands*. Napa: Val de Grace, 2008.

Schoonmaker, Frank, and Tom Marvel, *American Wine*. New York: Duell, Sloan and Pearce, 1941.

Shepherd, William R., *The Story of New Amsterdam*. New York: Knopf, 1917.

Sherer, Richard, *Crooked Lake and the Grape*. Bath: Donning, 1998.

Spooner, Alden, *The Cultivation of American Grape Vines and Making of Wine*. Brooklyn: Spooner, 1846.

Stiles, Henry R., *History of the City of Brooklyn*. Brooklyn: 1865.

Stokes, I. N. Phelps, *The Iconography of Manhattan Island, 1498–1909*. New York: R. H. Dodd, 1915–28.

Sullivan, James, ed. *History of New York State*. New York: Lewis, 1927.

Thompson, Benjamin F., *History of Long Island*. New York: French, 1839.

Thompson, John. H., ed. *Geography of New York State*. Syracuse: Syracuse Univ. Press, 1966.

USDA Special Report No. 36: *Report upon Statistics of Grape Culture and Wine Production in the U.S. for 1880*.

Van Diver, Bradford B., *Roadside Geology of New York*. Missoula: Mt. Press, 1985.

Verrazzano, Giovanni da, *Journal of Expedition*. 1524.

Von Engeln, *The Finger Lakes Region: Its Origin and Nature*. Ithaca: Cornell, 1961.

Wassenaers, Nicolaes van, *Wassenaers Historie Van Europa*, 1624.

Watrous, Hilda, *The County Between the Lakes*. Waterloo: Seneca County, 1982.

Wood, Silas, *A Sketch of the First Settlement of the Several Towns on Long Island*. Brooklyn: Spooner, 1824.

Journals and Newspapers

American Garden

American Journal of Enology
American Wine Society Journal
Bath Plaindealer
Buffalo Business First
Business Week
Crooked Lake Review
Dansville Advertiser
Dansville Herald
Eastern Grape Grower & Winery News
Fortune
Fredonia Censor
Friends of Wine
The Garden Journal (New York Botanical Garden)
Genesee Farmer and Gardener's Journal
Geneva Times
Grape Culturist
Hammondsport Herald
Inc.
Keuka Grape Belt
Methodist Magazine and Quarterly Review
Naples Record
New England Farmer
New York Evangelist
New York State Horticultural Society Proceedings of Annual Meetings
New York Times
New York Evening Telegram
New Yorker
Penn Yan Democrat
Pleasant Valley Fruit & Wine Reporter
Record of Horticulture
Cozzens' Wine Press
Horticulturist
Long Island Historical Journal
Long Island Wine Gazette
Practical Winery & Vineyard
Record of Horticulture
Rochester Democrat and Chronicle
Rochester Herald
Sommelier Journal
Syracuse Journal

Syracuse Post-Standard
Time
Vineyard View (Finger Lakes Wine Museum)
The Vineyardist
Wayward Tendrils Newsletter
The Westchester Historian
Western New York Heritage
Wine and Spirits
Wine East
Wine Spectator
Wines and Vines

Archives

<Archives.nysed.gov>
Cutchogue New Suffolk Free Library
Frank A. Lee Library, New York State Agricultural Experiment Station, Geneva
Fred and Harriet Taylor Memorial Library, Hammondsport
<Fultonhistory.com>
Glenn H. Curtiss Museum. Hammondsport
Kroch Library, Eastern Wine Grape Archive, Cornell University, Ithaca
Naples Library
National Agricultural Statistics Service
New York Agricultural Statistics Service
<Newyorkcorkreport.com>
Oliver House/Underwood Museum, Penn Yan
Steuben County Historical Society, Bath
Town of Irondequoit Historical Society
Town of York Historical Society

Index

187